IMAM SHAMIL

IMAM SHAMIL
The First Muslim
Guerrilla Leader

MUHAMMAD HAMID

The Other Press
Kuala Lumpur

© 2007 The Other Press and Islamic Book Trust, Kuala Lumpur

ISBN 978 983 9541 540

All rights reserved. No part of this publication
may be reproduced in any form or by any means
without the prior permission of the publishers.

First published 1977
Islamic Publications Ltd, Lahore.

Revised edition 2007
The Other Press *in cooperation with*
Islamic Book Trust

Published 2007
The Other Press Sdn Bhd
607 Mutiara Majestic
Jalan Othman
46000 Petaling Jaya
Selangor, Malaysia

www.ibtbooks.com

Cover design
Verso India Ltd.

Printed in Malaysia by
Academe Art and Printing Services
Kuala Lumpur.

Contents

Note to this Edition

Islam is a panorama of many splendoured things. In its long history, it has produced many great men in all spheres of human activity, the like of which no other civilization has produced in history: just rulers who were God-conscious and lived the life of their poorest subjects, great philosopher-theologians, scientists, travellers, historians, Sufis and builders of cities.

No less significant are such heroes who fought against injustice and oppression to uphold the dignity and honour of the community. One such figure in recent history was the Chechen mujahid, Imam Shamil, whose story will be a source of inspiration and pride for Muslims of all ages and lands who are struggling to liberate their land from invaders.

The Other Press in cooperation with Islamic Book Trust is planning to bring out a series of books on the great men of Islamic history and civilization. This book on Imam Shamil and his struggle against Russian colonisation is one of them, and this will, we hope, give the reader a new insight into the nature of a struggle against far superior forces by oppressed people to deny the oppressors the fruits of their aggression.

In bringing out this new edition, we have to acknowledge our debt to Mr Zaurbek Musaev and Miss Hajira Qureshi of Save Chechnya Campaign, UK, for their unstinting help in correcting many names of people and places of Chechnya.

Kuala Lumpur,
July 2007.

Author's Note to the
First Edition

First of all I thank Allah Who gave me the forbearance to write this book.

The years of 1831 and 1857 stand out in the history of the Muslims of the Indian subcontinent as . the years of great tragedy. A great hero of our freedom struggle, Sayyid Ahmad Shahid, fell a martyr along with the rest of his comrades in the year 1831 in Balakot. A chapter of our struggle thus came to an end, but efforts to oust the non-Muslim rulers continued and in1857, these efforts reached its climax. Ever since then British imperialism had to combat the freedom movement to put out the flames of our struggle for independence.

By and large the years between 1831 and 1857 have remained a quiet period. But at that time, the mountains of Caucasus were witnessing the struggle between the mujahidin led by Imam Shamil and the Tsarist armies. Although the story of their freedom struggle is not well known outside the region, this does not in any way lessen its importance.

The guerrilla bands of Imam Shamil taught a lesson to the Tsarist armies. A Russian general Valmeenov said: "The army we lost and the men who perished in these battles could have gained for us the areas between Turkey and Japan."

The great person of Imam Shamil has never been introduced as a guerrilla leader before. He encountered the best troops of Tsarist armies led by the finest generals of their time and yet he defeated them all. He was himself defeated many a time, but every time he reorganized his men and again brought greater number of troops against the Russians. He led his troops brilliantly throughout the different phases of war and utterly destroyed the great columns of Tsarist forces. Nowhere can one find such feats of courage, as well as examples of superb tactics in the history of guerrilla warfare. It would be only proper to acknowledge him as the first Muslim guerrilla leader.

I find great similarities in the many facets of Sayyid Ahmad Shahid and Imam Shamil's personality. The leaders of freedom struggle who were guided by the teachings of the Holy Qur'an have many identical aspects, as the mainstream of their thought and action was the same revolutionary spirit infused by the Holy Book. Sayyid Ahmad Shahid led a physically tough life. Imam Shamil had also become accustomed to the hardships and surpassed in physical strength even the hardiest mountain peoples. He excelled in riding and shooting and was renowned in the whole of Daghestan for these feats.

Sayyid Ahmad Shahid had tried for the eradication of common vices of society before waging his movement of

Jihad. Imam also combated the *adats*, the vices which had crept in society to such an extent that these had become prevalent. He inspired people to Jihad only after he had fought against the social evils.

Sayyid Ahmad Shahid found his followers amongst the common people. Imam Shamil also had his adherents amongst the peasants. We must pay homage to these brave mountainous people who waged war for almost half a century against the might of Tsarist forces—their homes were dismantled, their families burnt alive, but they never surrendered. Their gardens and orchards were put to fire, their fields were burnt to ashes and all their means of livelihood were thwarted and yet their spirits remained high as ever. Undaunted they faced all these tortures and privations.

Such, in brief, were the people who, with no outside assistance, with no artillery but what they could capture from the enemy, with no trust but in Allah and His Prophet (peace be upon him), their own right hands and flashing blades, defied the might of Russia for more than half a century; defeating her armies, raiding her settlements, and laughing to scorn her wealth, her pride, and her numbers.

The story which is going to unfold itself in the following pages recounts their deeds which though inspiring and full of the warmth of blood, have remained stored in the dead pages of history in dusty shelves for a long period. The Muslim world, and its intellectuals made no efforts to learn about him. However only recently there is again an interest in this heroic guerrilla fighter. Some books have appeared in Turkish language. This is the first attempt in the English language to represent Shamil in his true light. John. F. Baddley and Lesley Blanch have previously written about him, Baddley in a serious manner and Lesley Blanch giving rather romantic flavour to the figure of Shamil. Here is an effort to have a real assessment of the efforts of the first Muslim guerrilla leader, the one who defied the might of a great nation for half a century. The Russian armies with all their numerical superiority, resources and professional competence could not stand in front of these mujahidin who under the banner of Imam Shamil have left behind unique examples of their heroic deeds by prosing the truth of the verse of the Holy Qur'an. Many a group of smaller strength have dominated the larger groups with the will of Allah.

The stories of their undaunted spirit are written on the rocky mountains of Caucasus. These are little known to our people. I venture to write their history with a view that great deeds of their valour and sacrifices help to create the spirit of hope, courage and determination, in any sensitive soul. I would consider my humble effort fully rewarded.

It would be proper if I mention the circumstance, which led me to the writing of this book. Those who believe in a world of cause and effect may not attach much importance to it, but I consider it to be a spiritual blessing of the Imam that I was able to write this book. The Imam belonged to the Naqshbandiyyah order and was Imam of Tahrik-i-Muridiyyah in Daghestan. I myself owe allegiance to the Naqshbandiyyah through my late preceptor Mawlana Abdul Malik Siddique Naqshbandi (may God bless his soul) and thus I consider it a great honour that I could write about Imam Shamil.

I was sitting much depressed in the library of Pakistan Military Academy after the tragic fall of Dacca in December 1971, when I suddenly came across the portrait of Imam Shamil in a book. The gaze of his courageous face struck me. I glanced through the book and found much material on the Imam's life. Then I began to gather all the material, I could lay my hand on. Many a time, I had to ransack through the dusty volumes for a few lines. All thanks to Allah, that my love's labour was not lost and I finished this book.

The number of scholars and friends who encouraged me, and took genuine interest in getting this book written is very large. However it would be only proper to mention here only some of them. Dr Samad Shaheen, a great authority on Soviet Muslims, helped me by tracing for me some important books and always encouraged me. Mr. Abdul Latif Ulfat also lent me many books. Mawlana Abdul Quddoos Hashmi, a great bibliographer and librarian of Islamic Research Institute, Islamabad, and an eminent research scholar Mr. Mahmood Ahmed Ghazi, President, Council of World Muslims Affairs, went to all lengths to help me. Dr Riazul Islam, Head of History Department and Dr Mohammad Sabir, Head of Islamic History Department, Karachi University, also helped me. Dr Riaz informed me about a Turkish book in possession of Dr Sabir and sent it over to me. Major Waris Karimi who belongs to Turkestan, deciphered the contents of the book. Brigadier Syed Naseeruddin (at present Director of Army Education at General Headquarters) took great interest and encouraged me in this venture. While I was working on this book he was my head of department. Group Captain Inamul Haq,

Director Motivation, Air Headquarters and an ex-Library Officer of National Defence College, also helped in tracing out some important books.

Dr Ishtiaq Hussain Qureshi, an eminent historian of our times and ex-Vice Chancellor, Karachi University, wrote a foreword, and Maj. Gen. (Retd.) Fazal Muqeem, Pakistan's Ambassador in Saudi Arabia, wrote a preface. I am grateful to them for the kind words they wrote about me. Mawlana Zafar Ahmad Ansari, ex-Member National Assembly of Pakistan and Muslim World League, informed me about the address of Imam Shamil's grandson al-Ustaz al-Shaykh Saeed Shamil. He is a great friend of Mawlana Ansari and is at present living in Madinah. The Editor of Islamic Madniyat, Istanbul, Dr Zahid Baltaci, sent me two books on Imam Shamil in the Turkish language. Col. Faruq Siddique is a scholar of Turkish language and apart from my own platoon commander Col. Muhammad Azam, I owe him my understanding of military affairs for he was my company commander in the Academy. The staff of Pakistan Military Academy Library also deserves my thanks. I spent the best moments of my stay in Kakul in the library and it was there that the idea of writing this book struck me. The great historian of the subcontinent Mr. Sabahuddin Abdur Rahman, who is presently Director of Shibli Academy, Azam Garh, has been very kind to me. He went through the whole manuscript and improved its language and contents for which I owe him my gratitude. Maryam Jameelah has also been kind enough to read through the whole manuscript very diligently and offered valuable suggestions for which I must thank her.

Any mistakes or pitfalls in the book should however be attributed to me alone. I shall be extremely grateful, if the readers help me by sending me their valuable suggestions. I am now embarking on an ambitious project i.e., the compilation of Encyclopaedia of Muslim Military History in two volumes, for which I solicit the help of all those who are interested in such a venture.

Muhammad Hamid
Pakistan Military Academy, Kakul.
13 January 1977.

1
Geographical Situation

Before dwelling on Imam Shamil and his movement it would be proper to mention here the brief geographical location of the Kavkaz (Caucasus) and the places, the names of which would recur in this book. This will make it easy to understand the events of his life.

General Valmeenov who was commander-in-chief of Caucasus has written the following about the military importance of Caucasus:

> Kavkaz is like a great fortress, with natural defences as well as strengthened by artificial defences and military works, and furthermore protected by a large force. In this situation only a man having no understanding of military affairs would attempt to subdue it hastily. A wise commander would use his strength in a way as to clear slowly and advance cautiously in order to capture the fort.

Geographic location

The mountain range spreading north west to south east, between the Caspian and Black Sea is known as Kavkaz. The central mountainous range is an important part of it. These rugged heights have also contributed to the great qualities of head and heart which the inhabitants of these rocky ranges possess. It is difficult to conquer the peaks of these snow clad mountains and it is equally difficult to conquer the brave people who inhabit them. A Russian writer Lermontov writes:

> O Mountain tribes!
> Freedom thy God and struggle thy law of life
> Though have great friendship and still greater
> vengeance
> For you vice is paid by vice and virtue by virtue
> Your hatred like your love knows no bounds.

It can be said without exaggeration that these people were the creations of mountains. They fought so well that they had made these mountains almost unconquerable. While these high summits, narrow defiles and unpassable forests had infused a spirit of freedom in these tribes, it had also made their unity far more difficult task.

The total length of this long mountainous chain is 650 miles, out of which a purely hilly terrain spreads over 400 miles. The total length of the range along the Caspian Sea to Baku is about 150 miles, whereas the area to Black Sea is about 100 miles which is more or less a plateau about 100 miles wide.

The whole area which has been geographically distributed in three divisions, was similarly divided as far as struggle for independence is concerned. There is the forest-clad area from Albugz to the Black Sea coast and its average height is 10,000 feet above sea level. This is the area which is inhabited by Circassians who put up a heroic fight against the Russian invaders from the latter part of eighteenth century up to 1864. The tribes of Chechnya and Daghestan in the east continued to fight against the Russians during the same period. The tribes living on the barren plateau achieved great successes against the Russian forces but later did not face much resistance from the tribes living on higher peaks, where no pass is at a less than 10,000 feet. These tribes fought an irregular warfare but did not resist the Russians in any pitched battle. This gap between the two theatres of war could no be filled despite the best efforts of mujahidin and thus the Russian traffic from north to south flowed and this Georgian road created many difficulties for the mujahidin. One cannot understand the history of the period fully well without keeping this geomilitary situation in mind.

Georgians

Across the mountainous rough on the south are the people of Georgian stock (Stalin and his comrade Beria were both Georgians). Russian forces attacked and crossed these mountains on the pretext of defending them. These people always remained loyal to the Russian forces. Further south on the eastern side were the Muslim khanates[1] and the subsidiary states of Iran and on the west were the independent states of Turkish Pashas. Russian's designs were to conquer the western most tribes of Caucasus who had alliance with Turkey, and the tribes of Daghestan and

---

1. A 'khanate' refers to a political entity ruled by a Khan, or a chief.

Chechnya, unite the Georgians in Transcaucasia against Turkey and Iran and thus make secure its borders. Another aim of the Russians was to keep thousands of Turkish troops committed in Asia Minor and thus release the Turkish pressure from the European front. The Caucasian warfare continued for about sixty years during which period Russians had to encounter various Caucasian tribes.

Eastern Caucasus

The Arab historian Al-Azizi has named Eastern Caucasus as "the mountain of languages". According to him 300 languages are spoken in this area. Even if we consider this estimate to be exaggerated, we have to admit the latest researches which say that 40 different languages are spoken in Daghestan and all of them have no relation to each other. There is hardly any other place in the world where people, speaking so many different languages, are settled down in such a small tract of land. The dialects differ which ultimately leads to the growth of completely different languages. Various reasons have been assigned for this phenomenon. It is said that Alexander the Great sent here all criminals from his dominions. Land and climatic conditions here made it a place for the condemned. As the criminals came from different parts of the world, they spoke here many languages. The same was the case of the Andaman Islands being the asylum of those deported for life. Another interpretation is that various conquerors tried to rule this land. Most of them were defeated but then embarked upon reconquest. Consequently people from various parts of the world lived in these small but secure valleys. They maintained their individuality because of the lack of communication, their languages remained isolated and free from foreign influences. The same situation had occurred in Brazil where dense jungles resulted in a multitude of languages and tribes.

Area of Daghestan
It would be important to study the area of Daghestan in detail, as most of the battles took place in this very terrain. Situated on a high plateau the whole of Daghestan is surrounded by high mountains.

The highest summits, as in the Central Caucasus, are on the lateral or outlying ranges, the watershed or main chain from Shavi-kide (and indeed from Arkhotis-mata) to Bazar Diouai, where it rises to 14,722 feet, a distance of nearly 170 miles, being nowhere higher than 11,800 feet, while, the side chains are seldom under 13,000 feet, with many peaks still higher. The Bogos group, forming the watershed between the Avar and Andes Koisus and running north-east from the main chain, has at least three peaks well over 13,000 feet. Farther to the south-east there are two or more peaks of over 13,000 feet on the Dolti Dagh chain, with its outlier, Dioulti Dagh, 12,435 feet high; and still farther in the same direction, lie the Shall Bouz Dagh, 13,679 feet, and Shakh Dagh, 13,952 feet, the latter in the province of Baku.

There are two main river basins, of which the most important is that of the Soulak, formed by the union of the four Koisus—the Kazi-Kumukh, Dara, Avar, and Andy—of which the latter alone takes its rise outside the province, in Toushetia. All these run north and north-east in the direction of the range of the second upheaval, and all have worn channels of extraordinary depth and narrowness forming next to the chaos of mountains, the most characteristic features of Daghestan. The other system is that of the Samur, which rising not far from the source of the Kara and Avar Koisus, runs, though with a bend to the south, in a generally eastern direction, its lower course being now, as already stated, the boundary line of the province on the extreme south-east.

The total population of the Caucasus at the time of the war may be given, roughly, at four million; that of Daghestan at half a million, of which the Avars numbered some 125,000. Historically the most important of the tribes, and one of the most numerous, they inhabited a stretch of country more than 100 miles in length, from Tchir Yourt on the north to the border of Zakatali on the south, cutting Daghestan completely into two, and 45 miles wide at the meridian of Khounzakh. Their language is divided into two main dialects, those of Khounzakh and Antoukh, both differing greatly, from each other.

The Khounzakh dialect was spoken by the three Imams, Gazi Mulla, Hamzad Bek, and Shamil, as well as of all their principal lieutenants, so it became naturally the official language of Muridism,[2] and also the common tongue in Daghestan. This made the warlike and numerous Avars dominant.

---

2. Arabic which has been the lingua franca of the whole Muslim world and a great unifying force from Senegal to Timor, was a unifying factor between different tribes in this part of the world.

The people of Daghestan in selecting the sites of their towns and villages gave first consideration to their defence. So their choice was either great height or they were nearly always against the face of a ridge or rib of rock, isolated, or supported by inaccessible cliffs. They preferred to be safe against surprise attacks. The village of Arakanee is a fairly typical one. The houses were of stones, two storeys high, well built and convenient. The interiors were flooded with clay carefully smoothed and frequently whitewashed. They were built, as far as possible, amphitheatre-wise, so as to enfilade one another. The streets were made tortuous and barely wide enough for two horsemen to ride abreast; stradied, too, in places by a house furnished with a wooden barrier, making passage impossible until the defenders posted there had been ousted or killed. Nearly all these aouls[3] could be battered to pieces in half-an-hour by modern weapons from half-a-dozen different emplacements, but in those days they were either far enough from any neighbouring point of greater elevation, or sufficiently sheltered from them, to run no danger from plunging fire, such as could always be directed towards an enemy below. They could, in fact, only be taken by storm, and that was a formidable task when every individual house had its garrison of desperate men and often still more desperate women.

Since fuel was scarce, the next consideration was warmth.

---

3. An 'aoul' is a fortified village found throughout the Caucasus mountains, especially in Daghestan. They are generally built out of stone on faces of ridges or against cliffs to guard against surprise attacks.

For this reason the house invariably faced south, so as to benefit to the utmost extent by the sun in winter, while sheltered from the northern blasts by the rocks and cliffs behind it. All other conditions were of secondary importance, including even the extent of cultivable land in the vicinity, and the distance from which water had to be brought.

The various tribes of mountain in Daghestan differed from one another in many respects, but they all had certain characteristics in common. They are described as intelligent, patient, able to read others' minds at a glance and judge them at a word, strictly honourable, and living true to the ideals of Islam. In eating and drinking they were noted for extreme austerity and they took but little sleep. It is scarcely necessary to add that they were extraordinarily brave. They considered their martyrdom far superior to living under the slavery of the Russians.

Such were the inhabitants of the mountain of Daghestan, who fought against Tsar's forces. It must be borne in mind that the fighting took place for the most part in mountainous country, denuded of trees. Here the general level of the land was some thousands of feet high, with many ridges and peaks rising far above the snow-line: and that through this rugged plateau, the rivers had cut their narrow beds to a depth, generally of 3,000 feet and more. In the valleys or chasms thus formed the aouls are often hidden, and there the vine flourishes, and fruit trees, maize, and other cereals are grown abundantly. The irrigation channels and terrace work, that in places have made a garden of a land by nature so barren, cannot fail to excite the admiration of visitors from more favoured regions. There are scraps of cultivated land on many rocky hill-side of Daghestan to be reached only by difficult climbing, to which every particles of soil has been carried by hand; so small, too, some of them, that the anecdote of the Avar or Andean, whose field disappear while he slept, to be found again beneath his cloak, seems hardly an exaggeration.

Chechnya was the name given by the Russians to the region bounded on the east by the Soulak, on the west, roughly, by the upper Sundja, and on the north by the lower Sundja and Terek; while to the south its confines touched the mountainous countries inhabited by the Andeans and Avars of Daghestan, the Tousheens and the Khevsours. The whole country was, and for the most part is still, covered with dense forests intersected by numerous deep and rapid streams, having their sources in the mountains that rise upon succeeding higher and still higher ranges to the south. On the banks of these streams dwelt the Chechens, in isolated farms or in aouls, having sometimes hundreds of houses. The latter were one-storeyed, flat-roofed, built of sun-baked mud, strengthened with wood-clean and neat. They are mostly having comfortable paraphernalia: carpets, mats, pillows, and quilts, copper pots and pans, and other domestic utensils. Each house had its garden, or orchard, and round the aoul, in the forest clearing, stretched the cultivated fields, sown with maize, oats, barley, rye or millet, according to the locality. But, as the villages were unfortified, care was taken to keep one side over in contact with the forest, whither at the first threat of danger the women and children fled with all portable wealth. The forest, abounded in giant beech-trees which were their sure refuge and defence in distress against the advancing Russians. To it the Chechens owed much of all that went to distinguish them from their neighbours of the Kumyk plain and the Daghestan plateau. Just as it constituted the chief natural feature of their country, so did it mainly determine the nature and duration of the war for their subjection, a fact that will find abundant illustration in the following pages.

As long as there was the forest Chechens were unconquerable. The Russians made no permanent impression upon them except when they cut down the beechtrees and truly speaking they were beaten in the long run not by the sword but by the axe. Imam Shamil had realised fully the vital importance of the forests, and had given strict orders for their preservation. He imposed severe penalties not only for the wanton destruction of trees, but even when they were cut down, without his permission, for proper use. A cow or bull was the fine imposed for every trunk so felled, and in the worst cases the culprit was hanged for a warning to others. To destroy the forest was to destroy the defensive capabilities of Daghestan.

Every man was a born rider, a keen swordsman, and a good shooter; his arms—gun or rifle, sword and *kindjal* (dagger)—were his most cherished possession, handed down from father to son, generation after generation; and next to this arms, his horse was his valuable asset.

The Chechens were Muslims—though many a trace of *jahiliyyah* (paganism) were still surviving after their acceptance of Islam. There were mosques in the principal villages where teachers taught the Holy Qur'an. In Daghestan, and throughout the northern Caucasus, Arabic was the sacred language and it was also a written script. Until Imam Shamil's advent, all civil and criminal affairs were decided by the *adats* or customary law, and not by the *Shari'ah*.

Physically the Chechens were tall, well (though slenderly) built, and often handsome; alert in mind, brave and wise. Hospitality, as with all the mountain tribes, was-and is still-a most sacred duty; true to the traditions of Islam. Fighting against the Tsar's forces was the only pursuit deemed worthy of a grown up man, and the girls would prefer to marry some one who performed heroic deeds against the Russians. Household and agricultural works were left to the women-folk or to slaves, the latter being mostly prisoners of war.

2

The Movement of Jihad

Imam Shamil was not the founder of the jihad movement. He was in fact associated with a movement called Muridism and belonged to the Naqshbandiyyah[1] school of Tariqah. It was not merely a school which trained people in spiritual order, it also accomplished much in inspiring a spirit of independence in the people.

Mulla Muhammad of Yaraghi, (a village in the Kioureen district), may be considered as the founder of Muridism. This movement united Daghestan and Chechnya in their struggle for freedom. However he did not become the first Imam. This title properly belongs to Mulla Muhammad of Ghimry, better known as Gazi Mulla, who was succeeded in

---

1. Bahauddin Naqshband (1317-1389) was the founder of this school. 'Naqshbandi' means artist. Naqshband presented *tasawwuf* in its true colours, the school in Central Asia, Afghanistan, Turkey, Iran, Pakistan and India. All the schools of *tasawwuf* emphasise on following the way of life taught by the Holy Prophet. However Naqshbandiyyah pay special attention towards this aspect.

turn by Hamzad Bek and by Imam Shamil.

Gazi Mulla was born at Ghimry about the year 1793. He learned Arabic at Karacna, and completed his education at Arakanee, under Sagheed Efendi. He combined in himself in a rare degree the silvery voices and golden silence. Imam Shamil said of him that he was "silent as a stone", others had opinion about him that men's hearts were glued to his lips and with a breath he raised a storm in their souls. He excelled in the gift of oratory. He had a great influence on his people because of his knowledge and intellect. He was heroic, and single-mindedly devoted to the cause of jihad.

His comrade Imam Shamil lived almost next door to him as a child, and the two boys, who were destined to make the name of Ghimry famous, were close friends. At an early stage of his life Imam Shamil became noted for his extraordinary strength and energy, which he developed with all possible means. He practised swordsmanship, running, jumping and various gymnastic exercises until at twenty he had no rivals in these pursuits. It is related of him that he could jump with ease over a ditch twenty-seven feet wide, or over a rope held by two men of ordinary stature above their heads. He went barefooted and with breast uncovered in all weathers and excelled in daring and strength even amongst the brave and hardy mountaineers of Daghestan. He was quick, energetic, eager for knowledge, and proud but somewhat gloomy, and very sensitive.

Imam Shamil's first teacher was his companion Gazi Mulla, and he used to say that he learned more from him than from any one else. Both of them studied under several most learned teachers in Daghestan, and finally paid a visit to Yaraghi where they were initiated into the principles of the new Muridism. The first evil against which they set themselves was drinking where Gazi Mulla, began to preach. He asked Imam Shamil to give him forty strokes of a rod in public for having tasted wine before he had realised the enormity of such a sin, and Shamil in turn submitted to the same punishment. The crusade against temperance thus strangely begun had a great and lasting success. The people of Ghimry begged Allah, to forgive them. Many kissed Gazi Mulla's robe, and beat themselves, for their past sins.

The Russian bayonets
Meantime, while the circle of Russian bayonets closed in on every side Mulla Muhammad's influence had been growing year after year. The two forces, material and moving in concentric rings of opposite direction, kept equal pace, and just when outwardly it seemed that the last spark of liberty was being trampled under foot in central Daghestan by the soldiers of the Tsar, the flame had already ignited the land on every side, even to its farthest borders.

The exact dates of the events marking the early progress of Muridism in Daghestan are obscure but it seems that Mulla Muhammad was appointed *murshid* by Haji Ismail in 1822-23, and from that time he started preaching about the *Shari'ah* in the mosque at Yaraghi. Gazi Mulla began to preach openly at Ghimry in 1827, and he studied the Tariqah under Jamaluddin who in turn was taught by Mulla Muhammad.

Although he gave his daughter, Zeidat, in marriage to Imam Shamil, and was henceforth the latter's best friend and wisest counsellor, Jamaluddin refused to agree that the proper time of jihad had come, and even forbade Gazi Mulla to undertake it. The latter thereupon again went to Yaraghi, and addressed Mulla Muhammad as follows: "Allah the Most High in His book commands us to fight the infidels and the atheists, but Jamaluddin refuses to give us his sanction. Whose commands shall I obey?"

"We must obey the commands of Allah rather than those of men," was the answer and from that moment, it may be said, the decision was made. Returning to his native land he began to preach, insisting mainly on the necessity of restoring the *Shari'ah*, and abandoning the *adats* (pagan customs which had almost attained the position of law of the land) impressing at the same time on his hearers the political equality of all true believers, who owed no allegiance, he maintained, to any but those persons who were worthy of the favour of Allah and the confidence of their fellow countrymen. It followed that submission to the Russians was neither obligatory nor laudable, though permissible as temporary measure where resistance appeared hopeless.

Gazi Mulla was certainly not only an orator, but he was a learned man also, for he knew by heart over four hundred of the *hadiths*, or sayings, of the Holy Prophet (peace be upon him). He quoted these frequently in his lectures. He soon became so popular that even the old Shamkhal of Tarkou, a major-general in Russian service and loyal vassal of the Tsar, invited him to his capital, and allowed him to preach in the mosque at Kazanishchi and nominate a judge at Erpelle. Arslan Khan, of Kazi Kumukh, doubtfully loyal to

Russia, likewise received him warmly, and his fame spread far and wide in Daghestan. After gaining strength among the people at the end of 1829 he openly called on his *murids* at Ghimry to prepare themselves for jihad.

Social conditions

The greatest difficulty in the way of the liberators was not the power of Russia, but the weakness of their own country, which arose mainly from internal discord. Daghestan was divided into numerous khanates and free communities of many different races and languages, and for the most part bitterly hostile to one another. Inter-tribal feuding was chronic, not only amongst those various districts, but also in villages and houses from time immemorial. Their social conditions were almost the same which were in north-west India at the time of the arrival of Sayyid Ahmad Shahid in 1820. An elaborate system of blood-feud and vengeance, not only was sanctioned, but insisted upon by the *adats*. It might be illustrated by mentioning two or three cases to show the extreme types of primitive custom prevailing in Daghestan.

Imam Shamil told an interesting story about such blood-feuds: three hundred years ago, a villager of Kadar, stole a hen from his neighbour, who retaliated by taking a sheep. The first avenged by stealing two sheep, whereupon the second took the revenge by a cow. The original thief now stole his neighbour's horse, which so exasperated the latter that, finding no property sufficiently valuable to compensate for such a loss, he killed him and fled. Blood demanded blood, but the murderer was not to be found; so the relatives of the murdered men in default of the guilty one, and in strict accordance with the local *adat*, slaughtered one of his closest relatives. The blood-feud was now in full fury, and continued for three centuries, during which scores, some say hundreds, of innocent victims were sacrificed to maintain the honour of this terrible custom, and this was all for a hen!

In 1826 in another village, a fight took place in a room containing fourteen persons, and all but one were slain. The cause of the quarrel on this occasion was blood-feud which had already cost life. The *adats* varied considerably in details from village to village and tribe to tribe, but in principle they were the same. The passage in the Holy Qur'an related to blood-feuds is as follows:

> *And whosoever shall be slain unjustly, We have given his heir power to demand justice, but let him not exceed the bounds of moderation in putting to death the murderer in too cruel a manner, or by revenging his friend's blood on any other than the person who killed him; and O true believers, the law of retaliation is ordained you for the slain; the free shall die for the free, and the servant for the servant, and a woman for a woman; but he whom his brother shall forgive may be prosecuted, and obliged to make satisfaction according to what is just, and a fine shall be set on him with humanity. This is indulgence from your Lord and mercy. And he who shall transgress after this, by killing the murderer, shall suffer a grievous punishment.*

Surah al-Baqarah, 2:178

It need not be said here that the local *adats* were contrary to the laws of Islam as quoted above. Unfortunately, although the tribes had accepted Islam, they had not left the old *adats* of the period of Ignorance. When the grip of Islam loosened, these old customs again became the order of the day.

Promulgation of *Shari'ah*

Imam Shamil promulgated the law of *Shari'ah* throughout Daghestan. He punished anyone who attacked anyone except the murderer. Thus, the situation improved much. He also advised people to forgo the blood-money as it was desirable in the eyes of Allah. However these *adats* had taken such roots in the life of the people that except for the period of Imam Shamil, which is known as the "time of *Shari'ah*", these *adats* again got the better of society. Those areas of Daghestan, where the influence of the Imam was greater, still hold the imprint of *Shari'ah*. Conciliation is still preferred and blood money is agreed upon even now. Those coming back from pilgrimage to Makkah[2] add to the influence of the law of *Shari'ah*.

Lesser number of murders now took place in Daghestan, as compared to other areas in Caucasus.

The actual number of Murids was probably never great. We know that in the days of Imam Shamil's power, the fighting Murids were merely the immediate bodyguards. The total number never exceeded 132. However those who had gathered around the Imam were a highly selected elite possessing the first qualities of sterling character. They were the local leaders who infused the spirit of jihad into the

---

2. The Russian government had imposed ban on the performance of pilgrimage to Makkah.

whole of Daghestan. They were a vanguard and the brave people of Daghestan and Chechnya liked to march behind them.

Che Guevara, an expert on guerrilla warfare sums up this phenomenon in a sentence when he says, "The bond of guerrilla fighters is a nucleus around which the people gather and fight."

Jihad movement

Gazi Mulla's career from the date of his proclamation of jihad was brief and stormy, marked by notable successes as well as notable failures. Not for a single day was he oblivious of his goal of life. His first general appeal to the people of Daghestan in favour of jihad was written in 1829. After a public meeting at Ghimry, attended by religious leaders from nearly all parts of Daghestan, who with one voice acclaimed Gazi Mulla "Imam", and accepted his call to the jihad, it was determined to make the attempt.

Attack on Avar

It was decided to attack on Avar first. Its Khan at this time was a minor, but the government was in the hands of his mother, Pakhou-Beekhe, a woman of exceptional wisdom and great courage. On 4 February 1830, with a gathering of some 3,000 men, Gazi Mulla marched to Andy, where he was eventually joined by as many more. On the way he met with armed opposition from his neighbours of Irganai and Kasatli, but defeated them easily with a loss of twenty-seven killed and many wounded. He came all the way from Ghimry on foot, for he had not yet raised the standard of the *ghazavat* (holy war) and was so humble that he would not ride. From time to time he stopped and leaned forward, with his hand to his ear as if listening, though silence reigned on the mountains. When his followers questioned him he answered. "Do you not hear? I think it is the clanking of the chains in which the Russians are brought prisoners before me!" Then seated on a stone, he would develop his ideas and form plans for the Caucasus and take Moscow, "We will go to Istanbul, and if we find the Sultan a religious man, strictly obeying the commands of the *Shari'ah*, we will not molest him; otherwise; we will bind him in chains and his empire will pass to the faithful!"

When he drew near to Andy all the people came out, the Muslims of Andy spread out their garments for him. This episode had a great effect on the people in many places. In Avaria itself most of the people sided with the Imam. The situation at Khounzakh, the capital, a town of over 700 houses, was however difficult. Khounzakh decided to defy Gazi Mulla and defend the capital to the last. On 14 February 1830, the Murids attacked it in two bodies. They were commanded respectively by Gazi Mulla himself and by Imam Shamil. Their war cries were *"Allahu Akbar, La ilaha Illallah!"* (God is great, there is no God but Allah). The people of Khounzakh had never seen or heard anything so impressive. Their arms fell involuntarily to their sides, and the desultory fire they had opened suddenly ceased.

At this juncture, Pakhou-Beeke realised that the defenders were ready to give in, she used her womanly influence and came out with a sword in her hand. "Avars!", she cried, "you are not worthy to bear arms. If you cannot

afford to use them give them to us and take refuge behind
our robes." Stung by this bitter taunt the defenders rallied
just as the enemy were about to climb the breastworks. In the
fight that ensued the Murids were forced to retreat leaving
200 dead and many wounded. Imam Shamil was in danger
of being killed, but it was the first of his many narrow
escapes. He escaped because he was predestined to work for
Allah upon this earth. Gazi Mulla retired towards Ghimry,
giving out that this signal defeat was Allah's punishment on
the people for their want of faith and that they reform their
belief and practices.

Encounter with Russians
After taking possession of Khounzakh, Gazi Mulla wanted to
invade that part of Chechnya which was called Aoukh. He
attacked the Russians in their fort of Vnezapnaya. In return
the Russian commander, Baron Rosen, hastily marched to
the defence of that post with a small but compact force.
Hearing of the events at Khounzakh, he hurried on to
Mount Kharakhas, and there all the Koisubou except
Ghimry surrendered. Content with this he retired, and Gazi
Mulla felt relieved that the Russians had dared not attack
him.

In a few weeks he was again at the head of a large army
and got himself placed in a very inaccessible position at
Agatoh-Kala. An unsuccessful attempt was made by the
Russians under Major-General Prince Bekovitch to dislodge
him. This enhanced his prestige, so he marched with a great
number of followers against Ali Bonyon, and there defeated
another Russian commander, Baron Taube. After this he

destroyed Paraoul, the residence of the Shamkhal, (the local chief); captured Tarkou and besieged the Russian fort of Bournaya; which was about to surrender. But the Russians were reinforced at the critical moment; he was defeated with heavy loss, and, forced to retreat. He took refuge once more at Tchoumeskent. This was at the end of May 1831, and after ten days' rest he marched on Vnezapnaya, and laid siege to that stronghold. The Russian army, under General Emanuel, quickly came to the rescue, and the Imam, who had added much to his experience at Bournaya, retreated in time into the neighbouring forests.

When the Russians followed him there he inflicted upon them an exemplary defeat, capturing one gun, and wounding General Emanuel himself. The latter handed over the command to General Valmeenov.

Efforts of Imam Hamzad

On the other side of the mountains Imam Hamzad, (afterwards second Imam), succeeded in starting an independence movement amongst the Dajarobielokanis. In the course of its suppression the Russians, under General Strekaloff, suffered a severe defeat at Zakatali in which six officers were lost and 243 men were killed, 10 officers and 139 soldiers were wounded, out of a total force of little more than three battalions. Four guns were also lost, and to the bitter grief of Paskievich and of the Emperor Nicolay, both battalions of the Erevan regiment fled in panic at the very sight of the mujahidin.

Gazi Mulla once more retired to Tchoumeskent, where in August he received a deputation from the people of

Tabassaran, who invited him to come and lead them against the Russians in jihad. He at once set out for Derbent and besieged this fortress for eight days. He could not achieve much success here, so he made a daring and successful raid on the town of Kizlyar (The town was known both to him and to Shamil from their youth when they went there to see certain learned scholars as students of theology). The town was taken and Gazi Mulla returned to Daghestan with 200 prisoners, and war booty said to have been valued at four million roubles. General Kakhanoov was determined to destroy the stronghold of Tchoumeskent at all costs and after an abortive attempt on 26 November, Colonel Miklashevsky again assaulted it on 1 December. The place was stormed in spite of obstacles, natural and artificial, of such a kind that, the whole affair cost the Russians 400 men, though they had but to take a wooden tower defended by 200. Eight Russian officers were also killed in this attack including Miklashevsky. The Russians took back the cannon captured from Emanuel, but it cost them eighty men. One hundred and fifty mujahidin sacrificed their lives on this occasion.

In the mountain regions due south of Nazran, Gazi Mulla tried to unite the tribes of the Caucasus into one great Muslim state. To this end he sent a force of Daghestanis to spread the message of Islam amongst them. The mission was a complete success among these pagan tribes. The enthusiasm of the newly converted tribes was such that they murdered the Russian preestaff and a few other government servants and thus proved their zeal in the cause of Islam and freedom. To avenge this, the Russian army under Baron

Rosen, started for the mountains, General Valmeenov was his Chief of Staff.

The Ghalghais were too few in number and too poor to offer any very serious resistance; but relying on their mountain strongholds, which they imagined to be inaccessible to Russian troops, they defied demands for surrender and refused to deliver up those guilty of murdering the preestaff. The Russians formed a flying column at Balta, 14 versts[3] from Vladikavkaz, consisting of 300 regulars, with four mountain guns and 500 Ossietine militiamen. Since there were no roads, the troops took with them neither tents nor knapsacks. Each man carried besides his arms, merely a bag of biscuits, enough for six days. This was supplemented by a ten days' supply carried on pack-horses while a few men followed the column. Even the officers' tents were left behind after the second day. Three tents, for the commander-in-chief, his chief of staff, and chancery were however carried on. Crossing the Terek at dawn by a temporary bridge this small army began its march in column, but at the fourth mile already they came to dangerous abysses, the path grew narrow, the troops had to stretch themselves out in single file, and the guns had to be transferred from wheels to pack-saddles, so that in spite of its smallness the column was a long one, no less than five mile from front to rear.

On the fifth day, on the bank of the Assa, near the village of Zoti, shots were fired for the first time. There was no

---

3. A verst, an obsolete Russian unit of length, equals to 3,500 feet or a little more than one kilometre.

serious fighting, during the whole time the expedition lasted. Villages were destroyed, towers blown up, crops cut by the Russians. These freedom-fighters however knew better when to face the Russians in such force, and contented themselves with picking off stragglers or showering down rocks and stones on the invaders at various convenient locations.

The destruction of the last-named populous aoul was the final aim of the expedition, and the whole army now directed its march towards it. So narrow was the only path, that the troops had to keep their single file, and if one man halted all those behind him had come to a halt. This led to a humorous incident. Not far from Tsori a square tower of great strength commanded the path, and, garrisoned by desperate men, it stopped the Russian advance for three whole days. With enormous difficulty, a covered way was driven through the solid rock to the base of the tower and a mine was laid, after which the garrison surrendered. The Russians were amazed to know that their four thousand troops were detained for three days by only two mujahidin.

3

The Russian Campaign

Some time after the Ghalghais campaign Rosen and Valmeenov set out from Nazran with 9,000 men and 28 guns to harry all lower Chechnya. At that time (1832) the Russians had not yet cut avenues through the forests. In the early twenties, indeed, Yermolov had cleared a distance of a musket shot on either side of the road through the well-known Ghoityn forest, but this had already become overgrown by an impenetrable thicket of underwood, so that the Russians had to face warfare in Chechnya under the most difficult conditions. The Chechens merited the fullest respect as brave soldiers and amidst their forests and mountains no troops in the world could afford to despise them. Good shots, fiercely brave, intelligent in military affairs, they, like other inhabitants of the Caucasus, were quick to take advantage of local conditions, seize upon every mistake the Russians made, and with incredible swiftness use it for their destruction.

In war with the Chechens one day was like another. Only

at rare intervals some unexpected episode—the meeting with a large band, the storming of a fortified aoul, or a side raid—varied the deadly monotony of the proceedings. The Russians measured the length of the day's march by the distance between the clearings along the river banks large enough to allow of their camp being pitched a musket shot from the nearest wood. The road lay for the most part through dense forests of lofty trees, interrupted here and there by glades, streams, and gullies. Fighting went on from the beginning to the end of each march, there was the clatter of musketry, the hum of bullets; men fell; but the mujahidin were nowhere to be seen. Puffs of smoke in the jungle alone betrayed their hiding places, and the Russian soldiers, having nothing else to guide them, could only take aim by that.

After a march the Russian troops camped for one or more days according to the number of aouls in the neighbourhood that they were to destroy. Small columns were sent out on all sides to take on the fields and dwellings of mujahidin. The aouls blaze, the crops mown down, the musketry rattled, the guns thundered; again the wounded and the dead were brought in. The Tartars (the Russian allies) come in with severed heads tied to their saddle-bows, but there were no prisoners. The men took no quarter; the women and children were hidden beforehand in places where none dared seek them. The head of the Russian column returned from a night raid; its rear not yet in sight; it fought in the forest. The nearer it came to the open space, the faster grew the firing; one could hear the battle cries of mujahidin who surrounded and pressed on the rearguard from all sides; they rushed in, sword in hand, and waited only the moment in the clearing to pour in a hail of bullets. A fresh Russian battalion and several guns hurried forward to disengage it; the running fire of the infantry and canister from the artillery stopped the onslaught, and enable the column to emerge from the forest without much slaughter.

The Russian soldiers went out to cut grass, and at once a fresh fight started. Fuel for cooking purposes or for the bivouac fires could only be obtained by the Russians by great fighting. If on the far side of the rivulet there was brushwood or any semblance of a hollow watering-place the Russians had to cover that by half a battalion and artillery, otherwise the horses were shot down or driven off by mujahidin. One day was like another; that which happened yesterday would be repeated tomorrow; everywhere were mountains, everywhere forests, and the Chechens were brave and tireless fighters. They taught a lesson to the Russians who had encroached on their freedom and aimed at subduing their faith and free lands.

The order of march and disposition of the Russian camp were just such as best suited the circumstances and character of the war, and never varied. The column was arranged as follows: one battalion marched in front, one in rear, each with a few light field pieces, or, if the roads were unsuitable, mountain guns. The cavalry, reserves, artillery, and transport occupied the centre, and were covered by infantry marching in line on either side. In front of the advance guard, behind the rearguard, and on both flanks of the column for its full length went the sharpshooters, with their reserves and mountain guns. On the level or on open places three flanking lines or chains kept at a good musket shot from the column, but on entering a forest they marched as the ground permitted, striving as much as possible to keep the fire of the mujahidin at a distance, for it was too deadly when directed at a compact body of troops. The Russians called this 'carrying the column in a box'. On the march the whole of the fighting went on in the covering lines—in front when advancing, at the rear when retreating—and nearly all the time on either flank, where the hardest work and greatest danger lay. The sharpshooters, who went in pairs, often lost sight of each other in the forest and strayed; when the Chechens would rise as it were out of the ground, rush at the isolated couples and cut them to pieces before their comrades could come to the rescue. The movements of these mujahidin were seldom visible from the road followed by the column, as they were hidden by the trees and inequalities of the ground. The Russians kept communication by means of horns, signal numbers being given to the detached bodies of troops, rear, front, or flank, and these numbers frequently changed lest the mujahidin should learn to distinguish them. When it was required to know the whereabouts of any particular detachment or detail, a prearranged interrogatory signal was blown and the signallers of all the parties answered with their numbers; then judging by the sound, orders were given to increase the pace, halt, or close in, as the case might be. It sometimes happened that the bullets of the mujahidin found their way into the midst of the Russian troops, and they even sometimes succeeded in breaking through the chains of skirmishers and falling on the column itself.

The Russian camp was always disposed in a square, the infantry and artillery on the sides, the cavalry and transport in the middle. When the force was a small one, a larger was formed with the baggage carts. By day a thin chain of pickets was posted all round the camp, a musket shot from the tents. By night the number of sharpshooters was increased, the reserves were advanced, and in front of all, in dangerous spots, secret pickets were set after dark, lest the mujahidin should know their whereabouts. The strictest silence was enjoined on them, and they were not allowed to challenge anyone except by whistling, and they had orders to fire at the least rustling, even if uncertain as to its cause. On each face of the square parties were told off to reinforce the pickets in case of real attack. Three men lay down in front of the tents with their guns and cartridge pouches. The remaining soldiers and officers slept undressed and troubled themselves little about the bullets with which the Chechens favoured them nearly every night, creeping up to the camp in spite of all precautions.

On the eighteenth day, Gazi Mulla scored his last success against the Russians. Appearing suddenly in the neighbourhood of Amir-Haji-Yourt, on the Terek, he succeeded in drawing 500 of the Grebensky Cossacks some twenty miles away into the forest. After this he fell upon them suddenly from all sides, and completely defeated them. In this encounter the Russian commander, another officer and 104 men were killed, three officers and 42 men were wounded.

Six days later Baron Rosen—or rather Valmeenov, for the commander-in-chief left everything to him—stormed with little loss the aoul of Ghermentchoug, which was at that time the largest and richest in Chechnya, containing over 600 houses. Gazi Mulla sent a party of his Murids to defend this aoul. The inhabitants had no guns, so the attempt to defend the village in a nearly flat country against a well equipped army with artillery was of no avail.

The defenders displayed the most desperate heroism. At one end of the village there were three soldiers occupied by a devoted band of Chechens and the Daghestani Murids. The Chechens, who had shut themselves in the three houses and refused quarter, were firing hard, and had already killed a lieutenant-colonel and wounded several soldiers. Chief of Staff, Volkhvasky set out with Colonel Brimmer, commanding the artillery; Veiovolovsky and Bogdanovitch were to settle the affair in person. General Tornan was to guide them by the road he had already found through the village. The houses were surrounded by a triple chain of sharpshooters, lying down, behind the fences and trees. No one dared to show himself to the mujahidin, for the unwary were punished by bullets directed with unerring aim; and the Russians too lay down behind the fence, seeing no profit in exposing themselves as targets. The Russians brought up a light gun and the shot ploughed through the three houses from end to end. After the second round, however, people ran to say that the Russians were hitting their own people on the other side. If they cleared even one side of the sharpshooters and reserves it would open a way of escape to the enemy, and this was not to be thought of, so they gave orders to cease firing and set fire to the houses, if only from one side.

More easily said than done! In the first place, a layer of clay a foot thick protected the inner wattled walls, and secondly, the walls themselves were loopholed all over and bristling with deadly rifles. However, two Russian sappers were found willing to undertake the job. Pushing in front of them an oxen board of shield, and carrying bundles of straw and brushwood, they crawled to the narrow side of the end house, broke through the only foundation with great difficulty, and fired the wall, which began to smoulder under its fireproof covering. The Chechens continued to fire even from this side until the heat drove them from the burning wall. The sappers were now joined by a couple of artillerymen, also volunteers, who climbed on to the first roof by the burnt wall, took the hand grenades from the sappers, lighted the tubes, and threw them down through the wide chimney into the building, crowded thickly with the defenders. The first two grenades burst but not the rest, it was learnt later that the Chechens sat upon them out before the powder caught fire.

Little by little the fire extended on the remaining two saklias;[1] there was nothing left for the mujahidin but to surrender or burn. Volkhovsky was sorry for the brave fighter and ordered an old Mozdok Cossack, Atarshtchikov, who served as interpreter, to propose that they should lay down their arms, promising them in that case in the name of the commander-in-chief, not only their lives, but the right of exchange with Russian prisoners, thus giving them the hope of some day returning to their families. The firing

---

1. Saklias are cottage-like houses in an aoul, built of loose fragments of rocks.

ceased when Atarshtchikov went forward and called out in Chechen that he wanted to parley. The defenders listened to the proposal, conferred together for some minutes, and then a half-naked Chechen, black with smoke, came out, and made a short speech, followed by a volley from all the loopholes. What he said was to this effect: "We want no quarter; the only grace we ask of the Russians is to let our families know that we died as we lived, refusing submission to any foreign yoke."

The Russians now gave orders to fire the houses from all sides. The sun had set, and the picture of destruction and ruin was lighted only by the red glow of the flames. The Chechens, firmly resolved to die, set up their death-song, loud at first, but sinking lower and lower as their numbers diminished under the influence of fire and smoke. Death by fire is a terrible agony, such as not all had strength to bear.

Suddenly the door of a burning house flew open. On the thresh stood a human being. There was a flash; a bullet whistled past Russian ears, and, brandishing his sword, the Chechen dashed straight at them. Only to be shot in his naked breast. The Chechen sprang high in air, fell, rose again to his feet, stretched himself to his full height, and, bending slowly forward, fell dead on his bloodstained soil. Five minutes after the scene was repeated; another sprang out, fired his gun, and brandishing his sword through two lines of sharpshooters, to fall bayoneted by the third. The burning saklias began to fall asunder, scattering sparks over the trampled garden. From the smoking ruins crawled six wounded Daghestanis, alive by some miracle; the Russian soldiers lifted them up and carried them to the ambulance.

Not one Chechen was taken alive; seventy-two men ended their lives in the flames.

The last act of the bloody drama was played out, and night covered the scene. The chief actors had gone their way into eternity; the rest, together with the mere spectators, with hearts like stones, sought the refuge of their tents; and may be more than one in the depth of his being asked himself: why must such things be? Is there no room for the freedom lovers on this earth to live on their own without being disturbed by the imperialists?

The Russians turned the green garden red with the Muslim blood, happy homes of Chechnya into the debris. However the seeds of hatred against Russian nursed with blood still find their expression in the folklore of the area. The martyrs do not die and they still live in the hearts of the brave Daghestanis. Songs are sung in their praise and women narrate the stories of their brave fights to arouse the same sentiments in their children, which protected the mountains from the Russian onslaught in the past century. As a result of this expression the Russians could only obtain the temporary submission of eighty villages, the total destruction of sixty-one; the Russians loss one officer and sixteen men, eighteen officers and 333 men wounded.

Defence of Ghimry
Gazi Mulla now retired to Daghestan, and with Imam Shamil's aid he began preparations for the defence of Ghimry, for he realised the coming danger. He was eager for martyrdom.

After this gruesome experience, Gazi Mulla and Imam

Shamil knew the Russians too well to trust entirely to natural defence. Some five or six miles above Ghimry, but below the junction of the paths, they had built triple walls across the ravine, flanked and commanded on either side by breastworks of stone. The site was well chosen, and full advantage was taken of the natural strength of the position. Near the outer wall were two small stone-built saklias or houses. The Russians paid little or no heed to them never thinking that round them would centre battles of historic importance.

The two stone saklias were occupied by a group of some sixty Murids, who preferred to remain there till their death or till they had been cut off unexpectedly when the outer line of wall was taken under control. The main force of the Russians had swept onward, but two companies of sappers were there with a couple of mountain guns. Valmeenov himself, unknowingly, ordered the saklias to be cleared. After a few rounds from the guns the troops made the assault. The defenders neither asked nor received any quarter. They sallied out in one or two and died fighting heroically. Among them only two escaped, one of whom was Imam Shamil, whose marvellous strength, agility and swordsmanship helped him to save his life. He leapt like a tiger on the rear line of the troops, which was about to fire a volley of guns through the raised doorway where he stood. He turned and by whirling his sword he killed three of them, but the fourth one pierced his breast with his bayonet. Even then he took hold of the weapon with one hand and then killed its owner. After this, he pulled the bayonet out of his breast and escaped into the forest. Besides receiving the wound from it, he had his rib and shoulder broken by stones. After hiding for three days he managed to reach Untsukul, and there lay for twenty-five days more fighting for life against death. The Russian bayonet had passed right through one of his lungs. His father-in-law Abdul Aziz was a renowned surgeon who had also been in hiding. When he returned, he applied to the wound a mixture of wax, tar and butter in equal quantities which healed the wounds remarkably well.

The people of Daghestan, though not well qualified in the field of medicine, were certainly experienced in surgery, because they underwent frequent fights. They used to operate very successfully on all sorts of injuries, with the help of the *kindjal*, their national weapon. They would normally apply ointment prepared by Abdul Aziz. Russian officers sought help from them when their own surgeons failed to heal their wounds. It is said that they used antiseptics, though they did not know much about germs.

Martyrdom of Gazi Mulla

Shamil's escape, even if known, could at that time have seemed matter of little importance in the light of a discovery made ere the sun went down on the scene of carnage and chilled the October evening. Amongst the dead who lay so thick in front of the two stone hurts, attention was drawn to the majestic figure of a man. He was seen praying, with one hand grasping his beard, while the other pointed to heaven. When some natives were called to identify the dead they were greatly horrified and grieved. He was none else than their Imam, Gazi Mulla. His death was mourned by all. They looked at his body in disbelief. His dead body was taken to Tarkou, the Shamkhal's capital, and buried at Bournaya. Later on Imam Shamil sent a body of 200 horsemen by night, exhumed the corpse, and brought it back to Ghimry.

The Russian losses are officially given as one officer and forty men; nineteen officers and 320 men wounded, eighteen officers and 53 men contused. The Murids left 192 dead on the field of battle.

When Gazi Mulla fell, Imam Shamil lay struggling for life and the whole Murid movement faced a great crisis. At this juncture Hamzad Bek[2] was chosen as the new Imam. No important campaign or event took place during his time. Unfortunately Hamzad Bek was killed in a mosque by some conspirators.

Imam Shamil was then away from Khounzakh at this moment, but on learning the news of this assassination collected a force and went to Gtosatl. From there he further proceeded to Ashilta, where he was proclaimed Imam.

---

2. Hamzad Bek was born in 1789 at New Gtosatl, 12 miles north-east of Khounzakh. His father, Sikandar, noted for his courage and talents, raided Kakhetia many times, and was held in high honour by Akhmat Khan. Hamzad Bek learned Arabic and studied the Holy Qur'an first at Tchokh and afterwards at Khounzakh. When his education was completed he set for Ghimry, and joyfully welcomed by Gazi Mulla to became one of his most zealous and valued supporters.

4

The Era of Imam Shamil

The first important incident of Imam Shamil's period was General Fese's campaign in 1837. The army consisting of 5,200 troops, along with 180 field guns and mortars, reached the banks of River Aroma in early May. It had started from Temir-Khan-Shura and covered 27 miles in five days. It reached Khounzakh by the end of May. The difficult routes can be imagined from the fact that these 100 miles were covered in twenty days. Defences were constructed at Khounzakh. Four companies were left here and except for six guns, the rest of artillery pieces as well as heavy equipment was left there. Now General Fese left on 5 June for Untsukul and Ashilta along with two weeks' ration.

On the arrival of Russian forces the people of Untsukul had surrendered. They promised to return the Russian deserters and prisoners and surrendered hostages as well. There were quite a few Russian deserters in all the campaigns against the people of Daghestan. It used to be an important clause in all agreements made by the Russians with the local population.

On 17 June, Imam Shamil, Tashaf Haji and Keebat Mohoma attacked in order to break the night of besieging Russian forces after which a bloody battle ensued in which two Russian officers and 92 soldiers fell and three officers and 183 soldiers were wounded. The Murids also suffered almost the same number of casualties. About 100 Murids fell martyr in defending heroically and a good number of them was wounded. Considering the fact that the total number of forces in Daghestan was only 5,000, the Russian casualties were quite heavy.

Russian attack on Ashilta
On 9 June General Fese brought his forces at a plateau above Untsukul, and led them to attack on Ashilta. The Murid army had taken up a strong position on the left bank of the Betl, with its right flank protected by a high mountain wall, while its left side was naturally guarded by the abyss already mentioned. They were driven from the village which was their first line of defence. They contested every inch of ground as they fell back from ledge to ledge and terrace to terrace. The vines were besmeared with their blood. For three hours the battle went on in the vineyards and orchards, and then, at last the Russians found themselves face to face with Ashilta, in which it is said, 2,000 Murids had taken their stand after swearing on the Qur'an to die if need be in its defence. Fese collected his men and made necessary preparations for storming the aoul. He divided the troops into three columns, with the exception of one battalion and three companies retained to act as a reserve and cover the

artillery, which had fallen behind owing to the difficult nature of the ground. Two mountain guns, however, were soon brought up, and they took part in the attack. The left column was the first to reach the village, it faced a withering fire, and for some time it had hard work to hold its own, with its back to a wall of rock on the extreme left. Meantime the right column, under a very gallant officer, Major Fuchs, fought its way up the terraces to the extreme right of the aoul. It then turned to the left and began to fight its way through the streets. This relieved the pressure on the left column. Fese himself now came to the centre. The battle turned into hand-to-hand fight between groups of men on either side in and about each separate saklia.

The direction of the fighting slipped altogether from the hands of the commanding officers, and personal bravery and strength alone was decisive. The brave mujahidin rushed desperately on the Russian soldiers and died on the bayonets. More especially heart-rending was the scene of slaughter in the houses. No quarter was asked, no prisoners taken. General Fese followed in person all the incidents of the fight; he was seen now here, now there amongst the fighters, sword in hand. At last, towards 2.00 in the afternoon, Ashilta was taken and set on fire, but in some of the saklias the butchery lasted till evening. Driven from the village, the mujahidin gathered beyond it on the ridge, and encouraged by the cries of *"Allahu Akbar"* six times in succession flung themselves against the Russians hoping to retake the aoul; but all their efforts were in vain.

The mujahidin now retreated, partly over the Andy Koisu by crossing the bridge of Chinkat, which they burned behind them. They thus gave no chance to their pursuers. Some of them went towards the right bank of that river, while a third body took refuge on Old Akhulgo. The Russians lost 28 men, while nine officers and 107 men were wounded, one officer and 39 men contused; 87 mujahidin fell martyrs not counting the bodies burnt in the ruins, but many dead and wounded were said to have been carried away.

After completely destroying the aoul of Ashilta and all the beautiful vineyards and orchards, then in their summer glory, Fese intended to take up his position at Gherghebil, but he had not even started when 12,000 mujahidin who had gathered at Igalee, swooped down on the Russians and threatened to surround them. Fese succeeded in beating off several attacks on 15 June and at night retired to a stronger position, followed, however, by the mujahidin. The fighting was so close that when the flintlocks became useless owing to the heavy rain, both sides used stones. It was only at midday on 16 June that this "strategic movement to the rear" was completed, and the Russian army concentrated in its new position after an uninterrupted fight of twenty-four hours. On the arrival of three fresh Russian companies, which had left for Ghimry but had been recalled in hot haste, the mujahidin retired to Igalee and disappeared. The Russians had lost in this battle one officer and 32 men, six officers and 128 men wounded.

Russian attack on Tiliti

Fese retired to Untsukul. He received here fresh supplies, reached Tiliti on 26 June, and joined the forces where Imam

Shamil was defending himself.

Tiliti was a bit larger aoul than Ashilta—600 houses—and far stronger. Built on a stony platform, backed on one side by a cliff, while on the other three sides the only approach was steep and lofty rocks. It possessed unusually fine facilities for defence of a Daghestan aoul. It had no less than nine fortified towers. It had artillery as well in the shape of light falconets. After a few days the towers and many of the houses were knocked to pieces by the superior artillery fire of the Russians, and a storming party took possession of the smoking ruins, with a loss of one officer and 27 men, and one officer and 49 men wounded.

As fresh hordes were reported to be gathering for the relief of Imam Shamil, Fese ordered a general attack on 5 July. At daybreak the attack began, and when the troops reached the village all the horrors of Ashilta were repeated. The Russians had obtained possession of the upper portion of the aoul, while the Murids still held the lower part. When the Russian victory seemed certain, Imam Shamil sent envoys for seeking peace. Fese withdrew his men from their hard-won position and concentrated them on a high position. In the fighting which raged from the 3–6 July he had lost five officers and sixty men, three officers and 203 men wounded, besides some contused.

Negotiations continued for two days, and in the end Imam Shamil sent a letter to Fese, which was not happily worded for the Russian commander. Though not until already on the retreat, he sent a request that it might be replaced by another suitably worded. Shamil agreed to write another letter, but by this time he was obviously master of the situation, so the matter of the second letter differed little from the first either in content or form. The acceptance by General Fese of these letters, recording the conclusion of peace with Imam Shamil, was a political victory for the Imam as it confirmed in the eyes of the hostile communities his title as their political as well as religious chief.

Shamil's letters to Fese

From Imam Shamil, Tashaf Haji, Keebat Mohoma, Abdurrahman of Karakhee, Muhammad Umar Ogli, and other honourable and learned men of Daghestan. Giving hostages to Muhammad Mirza Khan, we concluded a peace with the Russian Emperor which none of us will break, on condition, however, that neither side should do the slightest wrong to the other. If either side breaks its promises it will be considered as treacherous, and traitors are held accursed before God and the people. This letter of ours will explain the complete sincerity of our intentions.

This letter explains the conclusion of peace between the Russian emperor and Shamil. This peace is marked by the delivery as hostages to Muhammad Mirza Khan— on behalf of Shamil, of his cousin, pending the arrival of his nephew; on behalf of Keebat Mohoma, of his cousin; and on behalf of Abdurrahman of Karakhee of his son—on that this peace may be lasting, on condition that neither side does any wrong or treachery to the other; for traitors are held accursed before God and the people.

Russian losses

This letter, however, was merely the pretext seized by General Fese; as a matter of fact he was compelled to retire by the total material disorganisation of the expeditionary corps, the enormous loss in personnel, and the want of ammunition. From the beginning of the campaign he had lost—killed, wounded, sick or dead of disease—four staff and 26 other officers, including 14 company commanders and about 1,000 men. The loss in horses had also been considerable, and half those remaining could hardly drag one leg after another. Of ten mountain guns, five were rendered useless. The wagons, and even the two wheeled carts (*arbas*) obtained from the natives for use in the mountains, had nearly all disappeared. The troops had worn out their clothes and boots and went in rags. Ammunition too had been depleted.

General Fese was a great master of the pen, and his report of the campaign was such as to gain him much brief renown and lead the authorities in distant St. Petersburg to think him a heaven-born commander, and once more to imagine that Muridism was now a dead force and Russian dominion in Daghestan firmly established. General Klugenau must have smiled grimly when he returned to Shura and learnt the truth, and one can imagine his feelings when in consequence of Fese's 'victorious' campaign he was called upon shortly after to induce Imam Shamil to proceed to Tiflis and persuade him to accept submission to the emperor.

Aftermath of Ashilta campaign

The defeat at Ashilta had ruined Russian prestige badly; retreat from Tiliti was effected just in time to escape complete disaster. The result of this campaign, as clearly evidenced by subsequent events, was not to destroy Imam Shamil's influence, but to increase it tenfold; for the Russians had left behind them a legacy of hatred in the ravaged gardens and smoking ruins of Ashilta.

The fact that Fese withdrew from Tiliti when already in possession of half the aoul on receipt of the first of these letters, and by a route dictated by Imam Shamil, makes it quite evident that the Imam had an upper hand and the Russian might was shattered. Imam Shamil returned to Ashilta, and his feelings may be imagined as he gazed on the desolate scene—the once flourishing aoul a mass of blackened ruins, not a house of the five hundred left standing, not even the mosque wherein he had been declared Imam three years ago: "I beheld, and lo, there was no man, and all the birds of the heavens had fled, and the once flourishing place was now a desolate wilderness." The vines torn up, the trees cut down, and the maize trampled under Russian foot, so that Shamil's growing influence might cease. The aggressors who gave no quarter, who battered down the house of Allah, who destroyed the growing crops, whose fury was on the fruit of the ground, could not visualize that the end was not yet in sight. Imam now went to Akhulgo and, having learned by experience, set to work with all his energy of his nature to make it impregnable.

The arrival of Nicolay

The emperor Nicolay was to visit the Caucasus in the autumn of that year, and so little did the Russians dream of what lay before them that it was thought that the emperor's coming might be made the occasion of celebrating the pacification of the Caucasus. To this end, however, it was necessary to procure Imam Shamil's submission; and secret and most urgent instructions were sent to the commander-in-chief, General Fese, to use all possible means to persuade the Imam to meet Nicolay at some point on the route, preferably Tiflis, ask forgiveness for past offences—which would immediately be granted—and offer guarantees for his future good behaviour. Fese, who was now in southern Daghestan, entrusted the conduct of the negotiations to Klugenau, who was as distinguished for his personal bravery and military skill as for his intimate knowledge of the local population.

Klugenau meets Imam

It is probable that Klugenau had no illusions as to his chance of success in so delicate and difficult enterprise, but the emperor's commands had to be obeyed. He despatched a letter by the Begs of Karanai demanding an interview with Imam Shamil, and the latter fixed a meeting after two days near a particular spring. On the morning of 18 September Klugenau, accompanied only by Yevdokimov, an escort of fifteen Cossacks of the Don and ten natives from the friendly aoul of Karanai, rode down to the spring, where he found the Imam already awaiting him with over 200 horsemen fully armed. The Russian leader, leaving his escort behind, took up his station on a little mound accompanied only by an interpreter, and asked that Imam Shamil should advance to meet him. The latter did so, surrounded by a number of the Murids, but on nearer approach the latter halted, and Imam Shamil advanced with only three of his most devoted followers. The representative of the mighty Tsar and the guerrilla leader were seated on horses face to face. They descended. It was a strange sight. On the one hand Russian soldiers were being commanded by a young adjutant who had received a wound on his face in encounter with mujahidin. On the other hand, was the group of mujahidin clad in robes of beautiful colours.

The Russian emissary exerting all his powers of persuasion. tried his utmost to convince, but Imam Shamil told him in plain words that he could give no final answer without first consulting his people. One thing was certain—there was no question of surrender.

An unpleasant incident

About 3.00 in the afternoon, finding Imam Shamil inflexible on this point, Klugenau rose to his feet; the Imam did the same, and the Russian stretched out his hand to bid him farewell; but, before Shamil could take it, his arm was seized by Surkhai Khan, one of the most devoted Murids, who with flashing eye exclaimed that it was not fitting for the leader of the mujahidin to touch the hand of a *giaour*.[1] Klugenau

---

1. A *giaour* (from the Turkish *gavur*) means infidel or non-believer, similar to the Arabic word *kafir*. The word carries the sense of hatred as that of *feringi* in the subcontinent. The word is still in use in the Turkish lands and carries the same hatred and scorn.

was already irritated at the failure of his mission, now he lost self-control and, raising the crutch he used, was about to strike off the Murid's turban. If Klugenau had committed this grave mistake, there was no chance of the Russian general's escape from this scene. In the battle that would have ensued, the Imam and his fellow men would have fallen and the whole course of freedom movement might have changed.

Imam Shamil, knowing the gravity of this situation acted promptly. He seized the crutch in one hand, and with the other held back Surkhai, whose *kindjal* was already half out of its sheath. He told the rest of his band, who were rapidly closing round, to fall back, and asked Klugenau to retire without delay. The latter, beside himself with rage, continued to shower abuses but the Imam exercised restraint not only on himself but also on his followers. Klugenau's *aide-de-camp* dragged him back by the skirt of his coat, and at last persuaded Klugenau to retire. Klugenau wanted to leave no stone unturned and wrote a long letter to Imam Shamil urging compliance with the emperor's wishes, but, this time, the answer was brief and decisive:

"From the poor writer of this letter, Shamil, who leaves all things in the hand of Allah—28 September 1837.

"This is to inform you that I have finally decided not to go to Tiflis, even though I were cut in pieces for refusing. I have many times experienced your treachery, and this all men know."

Imam Shamil now devoted all his energies to rebuild the shattered forces of the Murids for yet another encounter. He knew this was not the end of the road. He worked day and night to cement the ties of different tribes and clans. He also started the construction of his fortresses on the cliffs of Akhulgo, and had achieved so much power and strength that in 1839 the Russian government came to the conclusion that "it was necessary at last to take the most drastic measures against the growing might of Shamil."

Imam Shamil's authority was now recognised by all the free communities surrounding Avaria, including Andy and Gumbet.

Baron Rosen had been succeeded as commander-in-chief by General Golovine. At Count Grabbe's disposal were placed the whole of the military forces of the eastern flank and of northern Daghestan, the former to the number of 6,000 concentrated by 1 May at Vnezapnaya, on the river Aktash, the latter to the number of 3,000 a fortnight later at Temir-Khan-Shura. They first planned a combined invasion against Imam Shamil in Daghestan, and attack Chechnya in the autumn; for campaigning in the barren mountains was much less difficult in summer than at any other time of the year, whereas the contrary held good of Chechnya with its densely-wooded hills and valleys. But the skillful dispositions of the Imam's forces made all the plans of the Russian commander in vain.

Defences of the mujahidin

Tashaf Haji, reinforced by a party of Daghestan Murids under Surkhai and Ali Bek, had built himself a small but strong wooden blockhouse at Akhmat-Kala in the depth of the forest near Miskeet, an aoul on the river Aksai, and, gathering the Chechens from near and far, he threatened the Kumyk plain and the rear of any force marching from Vnezapnaya towards Daghestan. Imam Shamil himself fortified Arguani in Gumbet, and promised the people of Burtunai to advance and meet the Russians in Slatau. In these circumstances the Russians could not afford to advance without first securing the line of communication to the north and ensuring the safety of Kumyk plain, for which purpose they had to attack on Tashaf Haji's stronghold. The Imam ordered his forces not to put up any strong resistance, as a result of which the forces of the Imam remained intact. On the other hand, Russians had to suffer heavily in their retreat.

Arguani, like Tiliti and many other Daghestan aouls, was a strong fortified place and could only be taken after much bloodshed. The Russians had little mercy of human feelings for the brave mountaineers and it was at Arguani that one of the bloodiest battles in the history of Caucasian warfare was fought.

The Russian troops moved before daybreak towards the aoul and as soon as they had taken position, the aoul was heavily bombarded on all sides, after which the storming parties dashed forward and crossed the outer line of defences. Now the usual hand-to-hand fighting and slaughter in the houses and streets began.

At 9.00 in the morning, the Russian troops were already in occupation of the greater part of the village, and even of the flat roofs of those houses where the Murids still defended themselves; but the bloodshed continued throughout the whole day until dark. The only way to drive the Murids out of the saklias was to break holes through the roofs and throw down burning substances, and so set fire to the beams. Even then they remained many hours in the houses, though sometimes they found means to break through and secretly pass from one dwelling to another, but many bodies were found completely charred.

In spite of their unfavourable position they continued to do Russians a great deal of harm. The most brave amongst them were satisfied if they could destroy even some of the infidels; they defended themselves man by man with their sword and *kindjals* until they died on Russian bayonets. Some even threw themselves against a dozen soldiers at a time without any weapon whatever. Only fifteen men, who were being suffocated by smoke in one of the saklias into which the Russians had thrown hand grenades, surrendered. Many Russian soldiers perished when they tried to enter the houses; but the loss was far heavier—the streets were blocked with martyrs who had considered it more honourable to die rather than live under the shadow of Russian bayonets.

When night fell a considerable part of the village was still in the hands of the mujahidin. One tower in particular, which rose to the height of several storeys at the eastern end of the aoul, gave a great deal of trouble to the Russians. All the efforts of their infantry were in vain, and when evening fell they had to drag up with enormous difficulty two mountain and two Cossack guns, and place them on the flat roofs of the nearest houses in order to batter a breach. Even then the mujahidin did not surrender, and at nightfall the Russians had to take the most strenuous measures to prevent all escape from the aoul, especially from those houses still occupied by the mujahideen. It was night, indeed, that they waited for. As soon as it was dark and all quiet in the camp, they came out by secret passage and fled in various directions. Thus the fighting at Arguani lasted almost uninterruptedly from 4.00 in the afternoon on 30 May to daybreak on 1 June. The Russian lost 146 men (including six officers) and 500 wounded (including 30 officers). The mujahidin, on the other hand, suffered a great defeat—5,000 bodies remained in the Russian hands, of which 300 in a single gully where they were attacked by the Russian cavalry. The mujahidin had lost altogether some 2,000 men, either killed or wounded, and of certain villages not a single man returned. The whole village was burnt to ashes and the houses were razed to the ground by the cruel Russians.

On 5 June a flying column under Labeentsev, promoted with Pullo to the rank of major general entered Chinkat opposite Ashilta, and found it deserted; but the bridge over the Andy Koisu had been burnt by the inhabitants, and the position of Grabbe's army threatened to become grave if not desperate, for it was now cut off from its original base at Vnezapnaya, yet unable to effect communication with the new one at Shura, and meantime the provisions were nearly at an end, the country all round absolutely hostile.

Attempts were also made by the Russians to open up communication with Shura through Tohirkei on the north, but the people of that aoul, supporting the Imam, rendered these attempts abortive. In this emergency Colonel Katenine with two battalions, two mountain guns, and the whole of the cavalry was sent on the morning of 6 June to seize the bridge at Sagritl, five miles nearer than Igalee, but extremely difficult of approach. He succeeded in reaching it at 3.00 in the afternoon, only to find it broken down by the mujahidin. There were some houses near, and with beams torn from them the bridge was soon made passable again. By night both banks were in possession of the Russians, and next day Katenine marched to Ashilta. On 10 June, some dozens of sacks of biscuits were slung across the river on ropes to the hungry soldiers on the left bank, and by the evening of the next day, the bridge of Chinkat was rebuilt, the beams being taken from the house, and, for want of ropes and nails, bound together with vines. Grabbe, with the greatest part of his command, now crossed the river and occupied the terraces of Ashilta, the remainder took up positions on the bank opposite Akhulgo, except those who were told to guard the bridge, and thus the most famous siege of the war began.

Siege of Akhulgo

Imam Shamil was now surrounded in Akhulgo with a population of about 4,000 men, women and children. They were housed mostly in saklias built wholly or partly underground, and even in caves, not more than one-fourth fighting men, and herein lay the chief weakness of his position. For all must be fed, and as the siege went on provisions grew scarce while from the beginning water had to be obtained from the rivers at the base of the rocks, which could only be reached by breakneck paths down cliffs many hundreds of feet deep.

The Andy Koisu makes a bend enclosing, roughly, three

sides of a square. This square is irregularly bisected by the river Ashilta after its junction with the Betl. The right half of the square—New Akhulgo—is considerably higher than the left—Old Akhulgo—but both are several hundred feet above the Andy Koisu, which washes them on three sides at the base of steep, in place perpendicular or even overhanging, cliffs. Access to New Akhulgo is barred, and the whole promontory completely dominated by Surkhai's tower. Old Akhulgo reached from Ashilta by a razor-edged path, or from New Akhulgo across the narrow chasm bridged by planks at a distance below the double plateau.

Surkhai's tower, or rather collection of strong buildings on the summit overlooking the rock, was in charge of Ali Bek, one of Imam Shamil's bravest and most skillful lieutenants, with a garrison of about one hundred mujahidin who had exceptional courage and determination for the task. Some of these brave men had to descend each night to the brink of the Ashilta and bring back water for their comrades under the fire of the Russian sharpshooters. Surkhai himself was at Igalee, endeavouring to maintain the people of that important aoul in their allegiance to Shamil; Akhverdi Mohoma was in the Bogulial district, Keebat in Andy, on similar missions, for many of these people alarmed at the success of the Russians, were already wavering, and, left to themselves, might have submitted.

The Russian forces

With the battalion sent from Shura to guard the convoy of provisions, guns, and stores, Grabbe now had nine battalions under his command, but so great had been the drain from battle and sickness, that the total in the fighting line, including a company of sappers, amounted to no more than 6,000 men, the number of militia was about 3,600. With this force the Russian commander soon saw that he could not hope to maintain the blockade on all sides. Moreover, the position of the three battalions on the left bank of the Andy Koisu was one of considerable danger, one being practically isolated at the bridge of Chinkat, while the other two were down the river opposite Akhulgo. On 14 June, therefore, he withdrew them to the right bank, and for a time carried on the siege operations from that side only. Imam Shamil's position was thereby much improved, for the Koisu at one spot was so narrow that he was able to bridge it roughly with a few planks, and, during the first and second periods of the siege, renew his provisions, replace his losses in men and materials, and keep open his communications with Akhverdi Mohoma, Surkhai and others of his comrades outside.

Under these conditions Grabbe appealed to Golovine for reinforcements. The Samur expedition was already at an end, and the Russian commander-in-chief was in a position to despatch to Akhulgo three fresh battalions with four guns and a quantity of stores. When these joined the blockading force, which was not until 12 July, the total reached 12,000 soldiers.

Meantime Akhverdi Mohoma, Surkhai and Keebat had succeeded in collecting a large force for the relief of the Imam. On the night between 18 and 19 June, Akhverdi Mohoma quietly took possession of the bridge of Ashilta and set to work to entrench himself there, while the unconscious Russian headquarter staff were occupied in making a reconnaissance in face of Imam Shamil's stronghold. The danger for them was very great. Had Akhverdi Mohoma seized his opportunity, the whole scheme of battlefield would have taken a different turn. Unfortunately Akhverdi Mohoma let the favourable moment slip.

Attack of mujahidin

In the morning of 20 June when the Murids prepared for the attack, it was with loud reciting of verses from the Qur'an, and they began firing the moment they moved, thus giving the Russians the alarm and enabling them to concentrate in time. As soon as Grabbe had collected a portion of his forces he took the offensive; the ridge was stormed, and the mujahidin had to withdraw to Sagritl and Igalee. Now the Russian commander left General Galafeyev to contain Imam Shamil, and himself marched with four battalions and four guns, towards Sagritl and Igalee. At these two points the Murids kept some forces in observation throughout the siege. Imam Shamil profited, as expected, by the absence of part of the blockading army to make a raid, but it was not successful. The siege was progressing slowly, six batteries were erected. Moreover, a new and shorter route was opened up with Shura through Untsukul and Ghimry. A path had existed between these mutually hostile aouls, but had recently been destroyed where it passed under some cliffs overhanging the Avar Koisu. Grabbe sent a company of infantry to repair and enlarge it, but so great were the difficulties that it took from 27 June to 21 August to complete the work.

In this crisis in Imam Shamil's life the people of Ghimry

did little to help him. As long as communications were open by way of the left bank of the Andy Koisu they encouraged him, and some even joined his forces, but the majority refrained from actual hostilities, and towards the end, when Grabbe appointed Ullu Bek preestaff over them with full powers, they submitted to his authority and allowed uninterrupted communication with Shura. Like the people of Kufah, their hearts were with Imam Shamil, but their swords sided with the Russians.

Surkhai's tower

New Akhulgo was connected with Surkhai's rock, by a ridge only wide enough for one man to pass at a time. The siege works on this side were gradually advanced, until one night a company under cover of darkness succeeded in occupying a sheltered position at the near end of this ridge, and the rock was then surrounded on all sides. But the brave defenders continued each night to descend to the Betl for water. As long as this tower remained in the hands of the mujahidin, the Russians could not take the village. Then Grabbe decided to attack it.

At dawn of 29 June, three Russian batteries opened fire on Surkhai's tower. At 9.00, two battalions of the Kurin regiment marched to the foot of the rock; Russian volunteers dashed forward up the steep hill side (at an angle of 45 degrees), and rapidly climbed it in spite of a hail of stones and wooden beams became hurled down upon them. But the top of the rock consisted of huge overhanging mass several feet high. These Russian soldiers, however, did not stop even there; climbing on each other's shoulders, one by one they tried to reach the summit; but every soldier who came into sight of the defenders over the edge, under the very walls of the castle, went hurling back.

In the hope of lightening the task of the Russian soldiers the batteries from time to time renewed their fire in volleys; every discharge brought down vast fragments, stones and beams fell on the attacking party; but the thick columns of dust rising over the castle hid for a short time the heroic figures of the brave Murids. The moment Russian volunteers rushed once more at the steep ascent the mujahidin sprang out of the castle, showered down their stones and beams. The desperate fighting had already lasted several hours; one company had succeeded another, and at 4.00, two battalions of Kabarda regiment were sent to the attack but all Russian efforts were in vain. Only at nightfall and at the word of command did Russian troops retire from the bloodstained rock. The fight, which had lasted all day, had failed, after costing the Russians a loss of over 300, including two officers and 34 men.

The attack had failed, but at a heavy cost to Imam Shamil, for the heroic Ali Bek was killed together with many of his gallant hundred.

Then the Russians constructed more batteries and with the help of four new field guns which had recently arrived, they resumed the attack. On 4 July the castle was again bombarded, and, with the guns better placed and of larger calibre, it was soon reduced to a mass of ruins, in which the heroic defenders seemed literally buried. But whenever the stormers attempted to reach the summit, the dauntless Murids leapt once more on to the broken fragments of the wall and again hurled stones and beams upon them. The Russians knew that the place could not be stormed with success unless new tactics were used. They asked for volunteers from the whole army. These 200 soldiers were brought back under cover and ordered to wait for the night. Meantime the batteries continued their work of destruction until the greater part of the defenders were killed or buried under the ruins; the few who remained alive realised that further efforts were useless, and under cover of darkness tried to reach New Akhulgo through the Russian lines. The stormers at last penetrated the ruins of the castle, and found there only a few wounded mujahids. The Russian loss this time was twelve men including an officer, and 95 wounded.

The besiegers' task was now much easier for, no longer harassed by the fire from the castle, they were able to advance their works in various directions, especially towards New Akhulgo, and draw their lines much closer. New batteries were constructed, from which even the mountain guns could be brought to bear on the enemy's fortifications. The upper part of the ridges in front of Surkhai's rock was occupied by a whole battalion with two guns; another battalion with two fresh batteries was advanced nearer to the Koisu on the east; and on the promontory between the Betl and the Ashilta, two battalions were placed with a new four gun battery.

The Russians faced great difficulty in continuing the road or paths to the new positions, especially to the ridge in front of the rock. At two points, ladders had to be used, and at another where there was a sheer drop of 140 feet, tackles were rigged by which the guns were lowered and men in baskets. All this time the mujahidin under cover of darkness made continual sorties, to check which artillery fire was kept up all through the night. On 12 July, reinforcements had arrived from southern Daghestan, and allowing them three days' rest after their long march, Grabbe, judging that the siege had now reached a stage when Akhulgo might with advantage be stormed, gave orders to that effect on 16 July. The reports of spies had pictured the state of the garrison in the most lurid colours. Reduced in numbers, exposed to the midsummer sun on this barren rock, without cattle, for there was no forage, unable to cook their food for lack of fuel, driven by the continuous shelling to take refuge in caves and holes, worn by fatigue and privation, exposed to continual danger, and breathing in an atmosphere contaminated by decaying corpses, it might well be that, as stated, the dwellers on Akhulgo were no longer able to offer any serious resistance, and that Imam Shamil himself had thoughts of flight. But the event proved that both the local spies and the Russian commander had underestimated the courage and determination of their enemy.

The attack was made in three columns, of which the strongest, three battalions, under Baron Wrangel, was directed against New Akhulgo, the second battalion, under Colonel Prpov against Old Akhulgo, while the third, a battalion and a half, under Tarasovich, was to descend the gorge of Ashilta, enter the chasm between the two halves of the promontory, and henceforth endeavour to prevent the unification of the mujahidin's forces and in the event of success on the part of the other columns, to scale if possible the cliffs, and help to secure possession of the remaining positions.

From dawn till 2.00 in the afternoon was devoted to an artillery preparation; the troops were then moved into position, but it was at 5.00 before the signal was given for the assault. Wrangel's column at once made its way down the narrow ridge in single file under deadly fire, and with scaling ladders stormed the platform occupied by the first of the mujahidin's outworks, but here an unexpected obstacle confronted them in the shape of a second deep cutting across the ridge, swept by a crossfire from two concealed block houses. In a moment the position of the column became desperate. Exposed to a galling fire, crowded to the number of 600 on a very small space of level ground, with an impassable groge in front, a precipice on either side, behind them a passage so narrow that only one could pass at a time, and this already crowded with wounded men, they could neither advance nor retreat. They were soon without a single officer, every one had been killed or wounded, or had fallen down the rocks. The Russians were fortunate that being late in the day, it soon grew dark, for otherwise not a single man could have escaped.

The remaining columns, which were intended rather to draw the attention of mujahidin than press home an attack, did little or nothing. That under Tarasovich, after penetrating some way down the gorge, was met by a withering fire from Old Akhulgo on the left, while showers of rocks and stones started pouring down from the cliffs on the right, in these circumstances, and seeing that the main column had failed, it retreated. The third column made no serious attempt on Old Akhulgo. At dark all three returned to the starting point. The attack had totally failed, and the Russian had lost heavily—156 killed (including seven officers) and 719 wounded (including 45 officers); while the defenders' loss was comparatively small—150, but it included some of their bravest men.

The mujahidin fought heroically. Some women dressed as men, fought bravely in the advanced posts. The Russian commander had to face many disasters and great loss of lives, but he was obstinately holding the position and never considered over withdrawing his forces and leaving the besiegers to themselves. Although his pride had been humiliated he was not prepared to accept defeat. His ego might as well have forced him to continue the siege, but there were serious political and military stakes involved.

If Imam Shamil was left to himself, Russian prestige would have been utterly demolished and they would have never dared send their troops to the Caucasus. Moreover all the losses of men and material would have gone waste and the flag of Muridism would have flown high throughout Daghestan and Chechnya.

General Grabbe's new plan
The Russian commander had suffered a great defeat. Pondering over the causes of his defeat, Grabbe saw that a Russian victory was hopeless so long as the garrison could keep open its communications with the outside world. His spies brought him information that the day after the assault, a hundred fresh men from Chirkei and other banks from various aouls had joined Imam Shamil. He could see for

himself that new supplies of powder and provisions were being brought in daily, and that what was almost equally important for the garrison, the sick and wounded were being carried across the Koisu. On the other hand, in spite of recent losses, the Russian army was considerably reinforced and more advanced, and Surkhai's castle no longer existed. He decided to re-cross the river and attack, but to do so was no easy matter, for the bridge at Chinkat was destroyed, that at Sagritl was in the hands of the enemy.

Some days were spent in reconnoitering, it was pretended as if a new bridge was being built just above Old Akhulgo, and the enemy's attention having thus been drawn away from the real objective, three companies were thrown across at Chinkat on the evening of 3 August. The piers of the old bridge remained, and the river was soon spanned by a rough and ready structure strong enough for the immediate purpose. The next day, two battalions, together with the Avar and Mekhtuli militia, crossed to the left bank, drove off the Murids, and took up a position opposite Akhulgo, which was now for the first time completely surrounded.

The end was now in sight, though still a long way off. On the lower ridge in front of New Akhulgo two mountain guns, hitherto in a position wherefrom their great elevation they could do little damage, were added to four mortars already there. A new battery was constructed a little to the left, armed with four field guns but the most important work, and one that cost infinite trouble, was the construction of a covered gallery from the lower ridge to the counterscarp of New Akhulgo, with the double object of diminishing the loss

when passing that exposed position and allowing the
attacker in the next assault to concentrate secretly under the
counterscarp by surprise.

This gallery, devised and executed in circumstances of
extraordinary difficulty by the two young engineer officers,
Count Neerod and another, was a new departure in the art
of war, and has perhaps remained unique. It was composed
of a series of wooden shields made of planks and tightly
fastened together, and was hung by ropes over the edge of
an almost perpendicular cliff. A ledge here and there helped
to support it, and afforded space sufficient for sentinels to
guard the work while in progress. On the night of 20 July it
was partly destroyed by the mountaineers in a daring sortie,
after which the ropes were replaced by chains.

A whole month passed in this way from 16 July to 16
August, during which not more than a hundred men were
killed or wounded, but the sanitary conditions were bad, and
by the middle of August the army had dwindled again to
little more than 6,000 men, the battalions averaging no
more than 450 bayonets.

Meantime, however, Imam Shamil's position was growing
desperate. There was now no safety for anyone on any part
of the promontory unless in the caves, where some of the
women and children took refuge. Water could only be
brought from the rivers far below under fire of the Russian
sharpshooters, provisions were bad and scarce; there was
little or no fuel, and the air was contaminated by the bodies
of those who were killed or died of disease.

The August sun beat down fiercely on the barren rock,
and day and night the Russian batteries from all sides

poured in their iron hail. There was now no hope of any relief.

No wonder then that even Imam Shamil decided to have a truce. Djamala, starshina[2] of Chirkei, had long before offered himself as an intermediary, but had been informed by Grabbe that he would listen to nothing unless Shamil surrendered to the Russian government, and gave proof of his sincerity by allowing his son, Jamaluddin, to be taken a hostage. On 27 July negotiations were opened and for a few hours the batteries ceased firing. "In the beginning of August Keebat Mohoma, the well-known Gazi of Tiliti, offered to mediate, but this was rejected by Grabbe. On 12 August Imam Shamil himself sent an envoy to the Russian headquarters and firing was more than once stopped for a few hours. In fact the Imam wanted to gain time to repair his fortifications, and on 16 August an ultimatum was sent to him, to the effect that if his son were not surrendered by nightfall Akhulgo would be attacked the next morning. The storming columns were got ready, and when Jamaluddin did not appear, on the morning of the 17th, for the second time during the siege, Grabbe gave the signal for a general assault.

As before there were three columns against the defenders of Akhulgo, and the result was only less disastrous, for though by means of the hanging gallery the troops on the right reached the first outwork and there effected a lodgement, they were met, when they attempted

---

2. *Starshina* is a rank in the Russian military, equivalent to a chief of an army unit in rural areas.

to reach the second work, by the same deadly fire as before, and only suffered less terribly because the gallery enabled them to build some sort of protection. The Russian loss was already 102 (including two officers), and 455 wounded (including six officers), the remaining troops worn out with their exertions, and the whole of Imam's position was practically intact. Failure once more stared the Russians in the face.

Surkhai's martyrdom

The position of the Imam's force had, however, much weakened, as now exposed to an all round fire, they had suffered far more heavily than at the former assault. Imam Shamil had again lost some of his bravest and most devoted followers, and amongst them was Surkhai, who in all military matters had since been the Imam's right hand man. He was the same zealous mujahid who had snatched the hand of the Imam when he wanted to shake hands with General Klugenau.

The rocks were covered with dead, dying and wounded, the survivors were encumbered with the care of helpless crowd of half-starved women and children. Further resistance seemed hopeless even to the brave mountaineers. Imam Shamil considered any more resistance as suicidal and in an attempt to save the starving children and women, raised the white flag and sent his son, Jamaluddin, a boy of twelve years, as a hostage to the Russians. He in fact sacrificed his son to save his followers. Jamaluddin could only return after many long years of separation when he had become a stranger to his father and his people. The potential of a great mujahid had been shrivelled into a mere lieutenant in the army of Tsar. The Imam had all the time anxiously waited for his son. He was like the prophet Jacob waiting for his son Joseph to join him.

Negotiations

Grabbe now consented to negotiate and on 18 August General Pullo, with a small suite, was admitted to the rock, and had a meeting with Imam Shamil, whose conditions—that he could continue to dwell in his native mountains, and that Jamaluddin should remain at Chirkei in charge of Djamala—were unacceptable. Pullo returned, but negotiations continued for three days, during which it gradually became evident that Imam Shamil had changed his mind and decided not to surrender, and on 21 August the assault was renewed.

For the third time the Russians endeavoured to make good their entry into New Akhulgo, and for the third time they failed. The Murids held out as bravely as ever, and when night fell their position was still intact. Next day (22 August), however, at dawn, when the attack was renewed, the soldiers to their astonishment met no resistance, the outwork so long and gallantly defended was empty, and swarming into and beyond it they were soon in possession of the greater portion of New Akhulgo. At the village they found a few of the inhabitants who had remained behind while the rest tried to make their escape across the chasm.

Desperate defence

A desperate fight ensued, even the women defended themselves unarmed against whole rows of bayonets. Meantime the Russians brought two mountain guns and started firing on Old Akhulgo, where large numbers of the fugitives had not yet reached. Crowds of them were seen climbing the opposite cliff, or still descending the narrow and dangerous paths to the bridge of planks which, deep down as it was spanned the chasm seventy feet above the channel of the stream. The Russians on the plateau above followed in pursuit, and, at the same time, Tarasovich's column advancing through the defile, scaled the rocks, got possession of the bridge, and reached the surface of Old Akhulgo before the garrison was aware of its presence. In the two days' fighting the Russians had lost 152 (including six officers), and 495 wounded (including fifteen officers).

Akhulgo was taken at last, but the fighting continued for a whole week, accompanied by the usual horrors of Caucasian warfare. "Every stone rather every cave, had to be taken by force of arms. The mountaineers, refused all surrender, and defended themselves fiercely—women and children, with stones or *kindjals* in their hands, threw themselves on the bayonets. It is difficult to imagine all the scenes of this terrible struggle; mothers killed their children with their own hands, so only that they should not fall into the hands of the Russians; whole families perished under the ruins of their burning saklias. Some of the Murids, exhausted by wounds, sought nonetheless to sell their lives dearly; pretending to give up their weapons, they killed those about to take them. It was thus that Tarasovich died.

Enormous difficulty was experienced in driving the fighters out of the caverns in the cliffs overhanging the Koisu. The Russians had to lower their soldiers there with ropes. No less trying for them to bear was the stench of the numerous corpses which filled the air. In the chasm between the two Akhulgos, the men had to be changed every few hours. More than a thousand bodies were counted; large numbers were carried down the river. Nine hundred prisoners were taken, mostly women, children, and old men, and notwithstanding their wounds and exhaustion, even these did not refrain from the most desperate struggles. Some gathering up their lost strength, snatched the bayonets from their guards and attacked them, preferring death to a degrading captivity. The weeping and wailing of the children, the physical sufferings of the sick and the wounded, completed the sorrowful scene.

By the 29 August there was not a single mountaineer in Akhulgo. The soldiers of the Tsar had honourably completed the mission and duty towards the Tsar and the Cross.

The siege had lasted eighty days, and had cost the Russians 25 officers and 487 men; 124 officers and 2,291 men were wounded; a total of nearly 3000, besides heavy losses from disease.

A mystery

A question remained unsolved. What had become of the Imam? He was nowhere to be seen. The Russians searched every hole and cavern and corner again and again, and examined everybody both living or dead. He was nowhere to be found, nor could any information be obtained from the survivors that threw light on his disappearance. Had he flung himself over the cliffs like his sister Fatima and many others? Or, incredible as it seemed, had he effected an escape more miraculous even than that at Ghimry seven years before? It was not for some days that the truth became known, and even then for a time it was hardly believed.

It appeared that on the night of 21 August, seeing that all was lost, Imam Shamil, with one wife and child—another wife had perished in the siege—accompanied by a few faithful followers, took refuge in one of the cliffs above the Koisu. The following night the little party descended to the river bank, and constructing a raft out of a few logs, sent it floating down the river loaded with dummies to distract the attention of the Russian pickets. The ruse succeeded; the raft was luckily seen and made the target for many a bullet. Meantime the whole party crept cautiously along the bank downstream until they came to a ravine. Here they turned inland, but stumbled across a picket and a fight took place, in the course of which Imam Shamil himself and his little son, slung across his mother's back, were wounded, and the Russian lieutenant in command killed. But the line was broken, and hurrying on as best they could, the forlorn little group reached the upper valley, and, in what desperate plight may well be imagined, climbed the pass, and moving down the mountain side, reached the river bank once more at a spot a little above the junction of the Andy with the Avar Koisu, close that is, to the bridge of Ashilta, already mentioned. The bare sandstone here projects in huge slabs from either side so as to all but meet over the foaming waters, and the fugitives hastily bridging the intervening space with a plank, crossed to the left bank and proceeded to scale the mountain side.

They had not gone far when they were observed by a party from Ghimry who, had been sent to watch the bridge. Several shots were fired at them but without effect, and the Imam, seeing who they were, turned in bitterness and anger to his faithless fellow villagers, and shaking his fist at them, cried out, "We shall meet again, men of Ghimry!" then followed his companions up the rocks and disappeared from view.

The Russians misunderstand

Once more the Russians triumphed; once more the government in St. Petersburg congratulated itself on the destruction of Shamil's influence and the extinction of Muridism. Once more the medals were decorated; ball rooms were illuminated and toasts were proposed on the tunes of the sweet notes of music. Muridism had died and the looming dangers on the borders of Russia were no longer there. Who knew that the last cloud, which had disappeared in the horizon had all the potentials of many storms. The foolish hierarchy of Russia never knew that many a generation would have to undergo a bloodbath to ward off the danger from their borders. Many illustrious and brave sons of their aristocracy would succumb to the fatal wounds inflicted by the mujahidin and many a soldier would die unsung while attempting to subdue the forces of Imam Shamil. The Russians thought that even if alive, the Imam would be a mere fugitive hiding in jungles and mountains to save his life from the clutches of the Russians.

Within one year he was the leader of a people in arms; within three years he had inflicted a bloody defeat on his victors, and all northern Daghestan was conquered. Every Russian garrison was destroyed, and Muridism was triumphant in the forests and on the mountain from the Samur to the Terek, from Kavkaz to the Caspian.

5

The Imam's New Strategy
(1839-1842)

Count Grabbe was so satisfied with the immediate result of his efforts that he thought little of Imam Shamil's escape. Indeed, a price was set upon the fugitive's head. But Emperor Nicolay, who followed closely the affairs of the Caucasus and sometimes saw further than either his ministers or his generals, was not without misgivings. On the margin of Grabbe's report on the taking of Akhulgo he wrote with his own hand: "Very good, but it's a pity that Shamil escaped, and I confess that I fear fresh intrigues on his part, notwithstanding that, without a doubt, he has lost the greater part of his means and of his influence. We must see what happens next".

General Golovine wrote a letter to Colonel Pullo in November 1838 which read, "This dangerous man has been responsible for a great loss and we must endeavour to get him killed by every possible means. Many a brave men might be prepared to accede to our plan. Offer a sum of three thousand roubles to some of our confident men. The money will be paid immediately if success is achieved."

This letter shows that Russians had realised their mistake and were forced to offer greater amount of money for his head.

The state of things in Chechnya, however, during the winter months of 1839–40, seemed amply to justify even Grabbe's optimism. By his orders, General Pullo in December 1839 and again in January 1840 marched through the greater part of lower Chechnya, meeting no resistance. Grabbe attributed this marvellous change to his success at Akhulgo, and reported both to Golovine and to the war minister in St. Petersburg the re-establishment of absolute peace in the whole country: "Although we have not succeeded in taking Shamil, yet the death or capture of all his adherents, and the terrible sufferings of those tribes which supported him, have deprived him of all influence and reduced him to such a condition that, wandering alone in the mountains, he must think only of the means of subsistence and his own personal safety. The Murids' sect has fallen, with all its adherents and followers".

Dealing, moreover, with the plan of operations for 1840, he wrote: "Considering the present position of affairs in Daghestan and Chechnya it is highly probable that the expeditionary forces will meet no resistance, and that the building of the fort at Chirkei will be accomplished without the necessity of fighting. In Chechnya there is no serious unrest, and no general rising, need be anticipated."

The intention had been to build two forts only, at

Dacha-Barzoi, at the entrance to the lowest defile of the river Argun, thus initiating construction of the so called Chechen advanced line, Velimeenov's third Parallel. But as it turned out, only one of the forts was built—at Gherzel aoul.

Freedom movement in Chechnya

The spring had not set in when all Chechnya was once more up in arms. The Russians indeed played into Imam Shamil's hand in a way that even he could hardly have anticipated. Pullo was a brave and skilful officer, but, like General Galafeyev and Grabbe, he was a very cruel man, and what that must have meant in the Caucasus one can well imagine. He was, furthermore, quite unscrupulous, The Chechens feared and hated him, and when, failing to find the Russians sufficiently acquainted with the native language to fill the office of preestaff, he proceeded to appoint pro-Russian natives, who treated those subordinated to them with cruelty and injustice.

Their patience was soon finished. People were discontented and when the rumour spread—whether set about by the disaffected natives themselves or invented by the preestaffs for their own ends—that the Chechens were to be disarmed, converted into peasants on the Russian pattern and subjected to conscription, only a spark was needed to set the whole country ablaze. The people were ripe for rebellion; they only lacked a leader—the Imam was there to lead these mountaineers against the cruel Russians.

Six months had passed since the flight from Akhulgo, and the Imam had gained lot of influence in this period. He was received with open arms by his *naibs* Shuayb Mulla and Jawad Khan. Imam Shamil settled quietly in one of the smaller Chechen communities, where his influence soon became paramount. The fame of his wisdom and piety spread rapidly and, sending to Daghestan for Akhverdi Mohoma, he accepted to govern the affairs of little Chechnya on condition of absolute obedience to his commands, and rode from village to village preaching the *Shari'ah*. By the middle of March 1840, the inhabitants were up in arms, General Pullo had become alarmed and a rebellion had begun on the Sundja, not far from Groznaya (present-day Grozny), between his troops and the growing number of Imam Shamil's Murids. The Chechens were defeated, but the decision had been made. A month or two of Russian rule was sufficient to exasperate them beyond endurance; and encouraged by news of the disaster that had befallen their enemies on the Black Sea coast, and wild rumours of foreign intervention, they drew their swords again.

Until the end of 1840, the war had continued with even greater violence than before and soon it spread not only over the whole of Chechnya, but also a large part of Daghestan as well.

Guerrilla warfare

Imam Shamil, who had won his early fame on the barren mountains, now proved his mastery in that forest guerrilla warfare of which the Russians had already had a bitter experience. Avoiding whenever possible the danger of pitched battles with the disciplined troops of the Tsar, he moved about with great speed.

The great military genius which was portrayed by the Imam in all these battles, justified his title as the first Muslim guerrilla leader. He was to be seen at a particular place today only to be found at a great distance after a day. He was like a lightning, destroying the enemy and disappearing in the jungles moments afterwards. The whole phenomena seemed impossible, a mystery to the Russians, as he appears in the cold pages of history even today. He has not been surpassed in his superb tactics and his supreme eminence in directing guerrilla bands of Daghestan, is still to be marvelled at.

The Imam never wrote his memoirs and even if he had done so, it has never been preserved. It is a fact that there could not be any improvement upon his principles of guerrilla warfare. Whatever Che Guevara has written in his famous book *Guerrilla Warfare*, the Imam enunciated those principles one and a half century earlier in his own warfare.

Che Guevara writes:

> One should withdraw after dealing a heavy blow to enemy, wait, ambush, attack and again withdraw. This should be repeated again and again. Enemy should be relentlessly pursued.[1]

> The enemy should be constantly pursued. He should not be allowed to sleep in the battlefield. All his hideouts should be destroyed. He should be made to believe that he is encircled from all sides. These actions against enemy should

---

1. Che Guevara, *Guerrilla Warfare*, London: Penguin, 1968, p. 18.

continue in jungles and mountainous terrain.[2]

The principles, evolved by Che Guevara in the jungle
and mountains of Bolivia and Cuba, were not new. The
Imam manifested these principles in the mountain of
Daghestan much earlier. He had not been trained in any
military academy. He received instruction in the heat of
battlefield itself and excelled in the art of guerrilla warfare.
He can rightly be called a pioneer in this field.

He raided the settlements of Cossacks and punished
those natives severely who should not join in jihad. He
threatened, himself, within twenty-four hours, points 70 or
80 miles apart, while his lieutenants carried out the same
tactics to the borders of Daghestan on the east, to the
neighbourhood of Vladikavkaz on the west, thus keeping the
enemy on the alert, and wearing them out by the most
harassing of all warfare.

Grabbe at first refused to believe that his predictions
could be so utterly falsified. He remained far away, at
Stavropol, leaving Pullo to cope with a state of things which
was brought about mainly by the officer's own cruelty and
folly; and, later on, went to Pyatigorsk, sending General
Galafeyev to succeed Pullo. But soon the forces of the
eastern flank were engaged, and its chief was forced to take
the command in the field himself.

Early in 1840, after his brilliant success in Chechnya,
Imam Shamil extended his operations to Daghestan, where
thousands of Muslims flocked to his standard. On 10 July,

---

2. *Ibid*, p.21.

Imam Shamil faced his old enemy Klugenau; who having been reinforced in great numbers from Shura, cut his way through the mujahidin. Imam Shamil, for strategic reasons, retired across the Soulak. Shura and all northern Daghestan lay apparently at his mercy. On 14 September, Klugenau led his men down the 5,000 feet of precipitous road, past the well known spring, to Ghimry, and took by storm that birthplace of the first and third Imam. The taking of Ghimry was a sad event. However an incident occurred, the results of which in the long run compensated the losses of Imam.

Haji Murad

Haji Murad, who was destined to become one of the chief lieutenants of the Imam later on, was at that time loyal to the Russians. On the other hand, there was a feud between Ahmad Khan and Haji Murad. The former denounced Haji Murad in the eyes of Russians and pointed him as an ally of the Imam. Klugenau, believing the story of Ahmad Khan and receiving similar news from Major Lazarov ordered Haji Murad to be sent to Shura under escort, and put to death immediately if any rescue were attempted on the way. Accordingly, on 10 November the prisoner, Haji Murad, who had been kept chained to a gun for ten days, was sent off from Khounzakh in charge of an officer and forty-five men of the Apsheron regiment. The snow lay deep on the mountains, and as the main road was reported impassable, a roundabout way was taken and near the aoul Boutsro the path alongside a precipice was so narrow that Haji Murad and his escort could only pass in single file. His position, with two score armed men in front and behind, seemed to preclude the possibility of escape, but for greater safety a rope was tried round his waist, the ends being held by the two men nearest him. At the narrowest place he suddenly seized the rope in both hands, wrenched it away from the soldiers, and threw himself over the precipice. At any other season he would have been killed immediately; as it was, none thought it possible that he could have survived the fall.

Haji Murad, however, had courted on the snow, and not in vain. Although one leg was broken he was otherwise not hurt. He managed to crawl to a neighbouring sheep farm, and lived to become the terror of the Eastern Caucasus and Imam Shamil's most daring and successful *naib*. He was accused of conspiring with the Imam against the Russians. He proved that this accusation was right and helped the Imam in such a big way that the Russians trembled to hear his name in Eastern Caucasus.

The influence of the Imam

Imam Shamil dispersed his men; the Russian troops went into winter quarter; and, though fighting still continued off and on, the year closed quietly enough. But there could be no question as to the results of the campaign. The Russians on the whole had been successful in the field, but had nevertheless lost ground; while Imam Shamil, who had entered Chechnya twelve months earlier with only seven followers was now at the head of an entire people at arms, and an Islamic state had been firmly established from the borders of Daghestan almost to within sight of Vladikavkaz.

General Golovine's plan of campaign for 1841, approved by the Emperor, included the building of a fortress on the

Soulak, opposite the important aoul Chirkei, the inhabitants of which were to be severely punished for siding with the Imam. The defences of Shura were to be strengthened, a new citadel built at Neezovoe, and the old one at Khounzakh reconstructed. A Russian army consisting of some 12,000 men was to take the field. In Chechnya a slightly less numerous force was to march to and fro, devastating the land with fire and sword. A fortress at the entrance of the Argun defile was to be built. The troops in the northern Caucasus were reinforced by 14th Infantry Division, comprising sixteen battalions. The emperor, whose fears after Akhulgo had proved only too well founded, made known his expectation that the means thus put at the disposal of General Golovine "would produce corresponding results". However with all these forces and fortresses Emperor Nicolay was destined for the remainder of his life to little else than disappointment. Chirkei, indeed, was taken, and the projected fortress built; Chechnya ravaged. But, after eight months of irregular fighting, the troops went once more into winter quarters, Imam Shamil's position was stronger than before and the Russian situation had become increasingly grave. Especially was this the case in Daghestan, where because of Haji Murad's alliance with the Imam the Murid forces had strengthened.

Soon after his recovery from the effects of his fall, Haji Murad established himself at Tselmess, not far from Khounzakh, and, being appointed *naib* by Shamil, devoted all his energies and influence to furthering the cause of Muridism amongst his countrymen, the Avar.

Already in January 1841, after repeated attempts to win

back Haji Murad to his allegiance, Klugenau found it necessary to take serious steps against him. A force numbering nearly 2,000 men of whom half were native militia (irregular cavalry), left Khounzakh for Tselmess under the leadership of no less person than General Bakunin, commandant of the imperial Russian artillery, who happened to be in the Caucasus on a tour of inspection, and who, thinking that his experience would be not without benefit to the expeditionary corps, took over the command. Passek led the attack on the aoul on 6 February; all but one tower was taken, but that held out bravely and in the fighting that followed, Bakunin was killed.

The native militia held aloof, the Russians lost nearly a third of their number. Passek, however, managed to retreat in time to Khounzakh. Haji Murad's father and two brothers were also killed; he himself was wounded. The operations in Chechnya were resumed on 30 May, when Grabbe set out from Gherzel aoul with an army of over 10,000 men and twenty-four guns. General Golovine, then still commander-in-chief in the Caucasus, had narrated the following.

Dargo expedition
Grabbe's intention was to reach Dargo quickly, destroy that aoul then cross the range dividing Chechnya from northern Daghestan and subdue Gumbet and Andy.

At the same time the very magnitude of the force he collected for this movement served to impair its efficiency. He had with him, to carry his military stores and provisions, a large number of carts and some 3,000 horses. On the march, this baggage train, owing to the difficult nature of the roads, covered a distance of several miles, and to protect it even by a thin line of soldiers took nearly half the column. With a couple of battalions told for the advance guard and as many for the rear, and the rest broken up to form the protecting lines on each side, the whole force became extremely weak, having no men free to support the various units. Besides, it had to overcome very great difficulties, presented not only by nature but by the efforts of the mujahidin who quite understood that the march through the deep forests of Ichkeria gave them their one chance of success, and that once the column emerged from this difficult terrain they would be unable to do it any harm.

On 30 May the column made only five miles, though it did not face any opposition. All that night rain fell heavily, making the roads still worse, and delaying progress to such an extent that up to the evening of the 31st, after fifteen hours of march, fighting all the time, the columns had progressed only eight miles more, and was forced to bivouac[3] for the night on a waterless plain.

By the next day the number of mujahidin had increased, though according to trustworthy accounts it reached less than 2,000 owing to their main forces being with Imam Shamil in Kazi Kumukh. The road was yet more difficult, barricades more frequent, and for the second day the Russian troops were without water. There were already several hundred, and the general confusion increased hourly. In this way the Russian column made only 21 miles

---

3. A military slang, referring to a bivi bag, a lightweight alternative to traditional tent systems, designed to fit into a sleeping bag.

in three days, and General Grabbe saw that it was already impossible to continue the advance. On the night of 1 June, abandoning his enterprise, he gave orders to retreat by the same road. If the advance was unfortunate, the retirement was infinitely worse.

The Russian troops who had overcome all the difficulties of the advance, seeing that they had failed, and not being accustomed to failure, lost heart. The confusion and lack of control became extreme; no one made the proper dispositions, and no one troubled about keeping the column together. The retreat which necessitated the abandonment or, when time allowed, the destruction of everything that could impede movement, if only to save the wounded, the guns, and perhaps some portion of the impediments, assumed the appearance of a complete rout. There were Russian battalions that took to flight at the mere barking of dogs. In these conditions the losses were bound to be excessive.

This account was not exaggerated. In fact the situation had become so bad that it could not have been worse. The guerrilla warfare pursued by mujahidin had demoralised the Russians and broken them completely. Shuayb Mulla ordered the mujahidin in upper Chechnya to build strongholds on the back trees. These trees being so large as to accommodate about thirty or forty sharpshooters were ideally suited for the type of guerrilla warfare going on in Caucasus. These defences were so strong that even complete Russian battalions failed to destroy them.

At last, on 4 June, the Chechen column got back to

Gherzel aoul, having lost in killed, wounded and missing 66 officers and more than 1,700 men, besides one field gun and nearly all the provisions and stores.

Not satisfied with this lesson, General Grabbe undertook a second expedition soon afterwards, this time in Daghestan. Marching by way of Tsatanikh, he took Igalee, not far beyond Ashilta; but it had been burnt by the Murids. On the night of 28 June, General Grabbe set out on his return and reached Tsatanikh with a total loss of 11 officers and 275 men. The night retreat from Igalee was accompanied by the same disorders and losses as that through the Ichkerian forest, while the mujahidin's losses, according to Ahmad Khan of Mekhtuli, did not this time exceed 300 men.

In the course of four years, 1839–1842, the Russians lost in their expeditions, mostly under the direct command of Grabbe, 64 officers and 1,756 men killed, and 372 officers and 6,204 men wounded or missing, or a total loss of 436 officers and 7960 men, and had accomplished little or nothing. In 19th and 21st regiments not a single commanding officer escaped alive. By 1842, the regiments had lost more than half of their fighting strength.

6

Successful Expeditions

By the autumn of 1843 Imam Shamil had completed his preparations for a decisive campaign. In order to obtain the nucleus of a standing army, and at the same time keep control over the rest of the inhabitants, he had raised a body of armed horsemen, called *murtazeks*, chosen one from every ten households, whose duty it was to be ready at any moment to obey every command, in return for which they were provided for by the villagers, who had also to feed their horses, cultivate their land, and reap their crops. Nothing more admirably adapted to the end in view could possibly have been devised. Imam Shamil had organized in every aoul a select band of devoted followers, whose duties and privileges were equally to their taste. The *murtazeks* were divided into tens, hundreds, and five hundreds, under leaders of corresponding rank and importance. They were dressed in uniforms, the men in yellow, the officers in black, Cherkesses, and both wore green turbans. Leaders of hundreds and five hundreds, the latter generally *naibs* wore medals on their breasts with the inscription, "There is no stronger help than that of Allah". Other marks of distinction and medals were devised for those who were especially conspicuous for courage or good conduct; thus the famous Akhverdi Mohoma, first of the *naibs*, wore a sword inscribed "No braver man, no sharper blade".

The *murtazeks* were supplemented in time of need by an addition of one man from each household, who were placed under temporary leaders, and divided in the same way; while in great emergencies the call was made on every man in the aoul or the district capable of bearing arms. Those who performed heroic deeds received from him two bags of flour a month, and heroes on the front of their sheepskin hats a square of green cloth. Those who showed cowardice in battle were penalised by a metal ticket on their backs, if, indeed, they escaped mutilation or death. Cowardice was in very short supply in Daghestan.

The Imam never compromised on principles and was true to his beliefs. He did not spare anyone not acting according to the laws of the *Shari'ah*. Like Umar the second caliph, he had a rod in his hand to punish every evil deed. Had it not been for this firmness of the Imam, the superstitions and the immoral pursuits of the *jahiliyyah* could not have been uprooted so quickly. The policy of the Imam proved a great success and within a short period tremendous strides were made in the enforcement of the *Shari'ah*.

The Russian forces in Caucasus were in a miserable plight. Apart from their normal military training, they had to build forts and barracks, cut the forest and bring forage.

In extreme weather, they were given substandard food and had to suffer from hunger and cold. Away from their homes and hearths, deprived of their loved men and on the mercy of their enemy, many a time the soldiers resorted to desertions on long scale. In all these campaigns we hear of deserters. As a result of this situation, the entire body guard of Hamzad Bek consisted of the Russian deserters.

Guerrilla bands of the Imam

One great advantage of Shamil's military system was that it enabled him to gather or disperse his forces at will, and in an incredibly short space of time. His strategy and guerrilla tactics can be termed as superb and masterly considering the age in which he evolved them. From his central position at Dileem he threatened the enemy north, east, and south, kept them continuously on the move, dispersed his guerrilla bands to their homes, gathered them again as if by magic, and aided by the extraordinary mobility of mounted troops, who required no baggage, nor any equipment or supplies except what each individual carried with him, attacked the Russians continually where least expected.

The word 'guerrilla' is used purposely, for not only does it apply accurately to the forces led by his *naibs*, but Shamil's whole system of warfare. Long before the times of Che Guevara or Mao Tse Tung, Imam Shamil had evolved those principles of guerrilla fight which place him in front ranks of this mode of fighting.

In the present instance he had fully grasped the weakness of the enemy's position in Daghestan, and turned it to his fullest advantage. Like a good commander in the field, he knew the weak points of his enemy and took the best advantage of this. His plans were executed brilliantly and were crowned with great success. The Imam's old antagonist and the Russian General Klugenau, was no match to his genius.

On 16 August he reported that the Murid gathering had dispersed, and that all was quiet; yet on the 27th, Imam Shamil set out from Dileem at the head of an army, and in less than twenty four hours appeared before Untsukul, fifty miles away. Here he was joined the same day by Keebat from Tiliti, and Haji Murad from Avaria, each with a large party, the united forces amounting to 10,000 men. The rapidity of this long march over a mountainous country, the precision of the combined movement, and above all, the fact that it was prepared and carried out under Klugenau's very nose, without his even suspecting it, makes Imam Shamil worthy of the title of a great guerrilla leader. Judged in the perspective of history, the Imam may be considered as the first Muslim guerrilla leader.

The Imam had equipped his guerrilla bands with all the great qualities needed for this peculiar fighting. About the guerrilla fighter Che Guevara writes:

> He ought to be able to endure extremities, to withstand not only the privations of food, water, clothing and shelter to which he is subjected frequently but also the sickness and wounds that often must be cured by nature without much help from the surgeon.[1]

---

1. Che Guevara, *Guerilla Warfare*, London: Penguin, 1968, p.50.

The Murid forces led such a life. They had to face such situation everyday and had developed stamina to bear all hardship. They ate little and slept for only a few hours. They could ride for many days and survive the most brutal of conditions. The place from which Haji Murad had leapt was also attempted by a Russian guard only to perish there at the spot, whereas Haji Murad survived the fall. The Murids as well as Imam himself led a hard life. Even while he was under detention with the Russians and was provided with all luxuries, the Imam did not change his lifestyle or dietary habits.

The Murid forces were highly mobile and they could attack a far-flung place and reach back the same night. Their warfare was normally based on night attacks. Che Guevara writes in *Guerrilla Warfare*:

> The guerrilla combatant is a night combatant, to say this is to say at the same time that fighting requires. He must be cunning and able to march to the place of attack across the plains or mountains without anybody's noting him, and then to fall upon the enemy, taking advantage of the factor of surprise which deserves to be emphasized again as important in this type of fight.[2]

We find many an incident scattered through the annals of the Murid battles which explain the above quoted principles. The Russian commanders with all their intelligence and spying system could never locate the concentration point of the Murid forces and when they expected attack at a particular place, the Murid forces

---

2. *Ibid*, p.48.

attacked a point about seventy or eighty miles away and disappeared during the same night. They normally attacked when the Russians marched in columns, and inflicted heavy losses on them. Che Guevara writes:

> An entrenched enemy is never the favourite prey of the guerrilla fighter. He prefers his enemy to be on the move, nervous, not knowing the ground, fearful of everything and without natural protections for defence.[3]

A successful commander

Like every experienced military leader, Imam Shamil knew all the weaknesses of enemy positions. He shattered the might of the Russian army as he was aware of all the loopholes in the enemy forces. The Russian forces were divided into small units scattered throughout Daghestan. These insecure and weak forces, torn apart from each other, were an easy prey for the Imam's guerrilla bands. He had realised that the enemy could be countered in this way.

He organized his campaigns, planned them so well and collected all necessary intelligence about enemy forces so completely that no chief-of-staff could accomplish it with the help of many staff officers. A team of officers under the guidance of commander-in-chief and chief-of-staff was planning the war scheme and these were the veteran officers who were professionally sound, had many rows of ribbons on their chests and who had all the resources of artillery, armour, infantry and were knocking their heads against the citadel of Daghestan for the past half a century.

---

3. *Ibid.*, p.54.

Arrayed against them were the resourceless mujahidin of Daghestan who had no artillery or other sophisticated armaments. They lacked in equipment and had not been trained in war academies, never planned battles in the operation rooms with the help of maps and did not have the experience of fighting on the many battle fronts like Tsarist armies—and yet they had thwarted all the designs of Russian armies for a prolonged period. All the might of Tsar's army perished in the mountains of Caucasus could not subdue the bold spirits of these brave mountaineers. Many an illustrious son of the magnificent families succumbed to their last in the mountainous fastness of Daghestan and many a heap of Russian corpses filled the gaps in the rocks and yet without any gain.

The Imam's superb personality
Apart from other reasons of the Murids' successes, the Imam's superb personality was a factor of great importance. The Imam's foresight and military acumen helped Daghestanis achieve great successes against the Tsarist forces. The main adversary of the Imam, General Klegenau, could never assess the military genius of the Imam. He had led many battles against the Imam and yet he could not correctly gauge the essential skill and the capabilities of the Imam and his forces.

An interesting incident may be mentioned here. On 16 August 1843, Klegenau sent a report to the Russian headquarters that the Murid forces have been destroyed and that law and order had been restored. Only eleven days after this report the Imam advanced from Veleem at the head of a large army and within twenty four hours reached Untsukul where Keebat Mohoma from Tiliti and Haji Murad from Avaria joined him with their columns. The total strength of the Imam's forces had now reached ten thousand. Crossing the mountain chains over such a long stretch and reaching at the same time shows the superb ability of the Imam. It may be mentioned that it all happened right under Klegenau's nose, and that he could not check any of these advances speaks volumes for the genius of the Imam.

Imam Shamil can be counted in the first rank commanders in the annals of world military history. Such epithets like a high ranking guerrilla leader cannot describe him. It would be no exaggeration to say that history cannot present a single commander above his calibre.

None can raise a finger on the bravery of the Russian soldiers or the brilliance of their officers. They fought recklessly. Their generals did not study maps in the operation rooms. Many of them fell in the battlefields. One cannot pass any comment on their character or valour. No doubt they were the best soldiers of Tsar's army, and yet they pale into comparison with the genius of the Imam. About a dozen generals fought against the Imam one after another. The commanders enjoying a fine professional standing encountered the forces of the Imam and yet each one of them was defeated. Many times the Imam had no chance of survival, his comrades were all dead and as the Russians put it, the movement was crushed, the whole of Daghestan had been destroyed by sword and fire. The harrowing tales of Russian barbarism had struck a terror in the hearts of the people.

And yet the same people who fled away at a single fire of Russian artillery had within a short period killed the chief of Russian artillery and were not ready to accept defeat even after weeks of unremitting artillery fire. It was the magnetic personality of the Imam, which had made these people withstand the might of the Russian onslaught so bravely and blunt their attacks.

One fails to interpret these events in the light of history. The Imam was a fire which had devoured the Tsarist armies by thousands. Every general had to face a new defeat and every new commander was forced to revise his estimates.

The surrender of Untsukul

The inhabitants of Untsukul had revolted against the Imam. They had handed over 78 Murids of the Imam to the Russian commander the year before and had allowed the Russians to camp in their village and construct a cantonment. It was important to teach these unfaithful people a lesson, and make them pay the cost of betrayal to the Imam. The Imam decided to crush these rebels and planned to destroy the cantonment as well as punish these people for their betrayal. He completed the whole task thoroughly.

When Colonel Vesselitsky at Ghimry heard of the Imam's approach, he hurried out without waiting for instructions, with the object of saving Untsukul. He was joined on the way by Major Grabovsky, who, equally without authority, had brought with him part of the garrison of Tsatanikh on the same mission. They now picked up two more companies at Kharachee, and with this combined force of more than 500 men along with two guns, Vesselitsky marched on Utsukul. On the morning of 29 August, leaving his guns on the height above the aoul, he descended into the gardens, and tried to gain possession of them, but was driven back with heavy loss.

Meantime the enemy had outflanked him, stormed the heights, and taken possession of the guns. The unhappy remnant of the Russians was immediately surrounded, and was driven in disorder to the river bank. Vesselitsky was taken prisoner, Grabovsky, Schultz, nine other officers and 477 men were killed; of the entire force only a few men could escape by swimming across the Koisu. Yevdokimov, who had been sent off in hot haste by Klugenau to Tsatanikh, was prevented by the rash movements of the above-mentioned officers, and witnessed their destruction from afar without being able to help them. Two days later the garrison of the Russian fort surrendered to Imam Shamil, who was very impressed by the heroic defence of the Russian fort and returned the sword back to Lieutenant Ansov for leading the defence of the fort so bravely. The Imam had stormed the aoul and captured it.

The rescue of Klugenau

In the meantime Klugenau, had reached Tsatnikh, and there had gathered a force of 1,100 men. The important position of Kharachee had been entrusted to Major Kossovich with 210 regulars and some native militia, with instructions not to leave it on any consideration. Nevertheless, on the approach of Imam Shamil, he was so frightened that he abandoned his post without waiting to be attacked, and retired to Balakhani. The first result was a brave but unsuccessful attempt to retake Kharachee; in which the leader, Major Zaitsev, eight other officers, and 110 men were killed, three officers and 68 men wounded. Klugenau's communications with Shura were now in great danger, and, having to choose between retiring to Balakhani to guard them and attempting to save the garrisons in Avaria, he decided in favour of the latter course, and, abandoning his base, made his way to Khounzakh. There he was surrounded and besieged by Imam Shamil until relieved on 14 September by Major General Prince Argutinsky-Dolgoroukov, who fought his way up from southern Daghestan on hearing the desperate condition of his superior officer. The combined forces at Khounzakh now totalled over 6,000, but they were unable to harm the forces of the Imam.

The surrender of Russian forts

Meantime, within twenty five days from his sudden appearance before Untsukul (27 August to 21 September), Imam Shamil had captured all the Russian fortified places in Avaria except the capital, together with 14 guns; and the Russians had lost in the same short space of time, 65 officers and 1,999 men—either killed, wounded or taken prisoner.

Akhalchi had been surrendered in a most cowardly way by the officer in command without firing a shot; Kharachee was abandoned. However, at two other places the Russian army fought desperately against the Murid forces.

Imam Shamil did not attack the Russians at Khounzakh, though Haji Murad had urged him to do so. The withdrawal of the Russians from Avaria could be achieved in another way with no such risk, and Imam Shamil was too experienced a general not to know this. He retired to Chinkat, and thence to Dileem, and on 30 September attacked on Andreyevo and the adjoining fort, Vnezapnaya. The attempt failed owing to the courage and resourcefulness of the Russian commander, Colonel Kozlovsky. Imam Shamil then dismissed his men to their homes, but his reappearance at Dileem had made it impossible for the Russians to keep the bulk of their forces shut up in Avaria, and Klugenau, therefore, returned to Shura on 28 September, leaving Passek in garrison at Khounzakh with four battalions, Argutinsky at Balakhani with as many more and his Kouba native militia, to guard the defile. Two weeks later, the last named General retired to southern Daghestan, leaving, apparently, only one and a half battalions distributed between Balakhani and Ziriani.

There were now in northern Daghestan at the disposal of Lieutenant General Gourko, who had taken over the supreme command, 17 battalions counting 9,000 bayonets, and eight *sotnias*[4] of cavalry. However, two fatal mistakes had been made by the Russians and Imam Shamil's eagle eye did not fail to note them. The important post of Gherghebil was garrisoned by only 306 men of the Tiflis regiment, with a few artillerymen, Nouroundouk Kale, the watchtower on the height between the Irganai defile and Shura, with its handful of men, was also completely forgotten! Yet these two points commanded the only available routes between Shura

---

4. A combat unit used by the Russian army. A *sotnia* contained three or four platoons.

and Avaria, and, once occupied, Passek's force and the garrisons at Balakhani and Ziriani could be completely isolated.

It was in the middle of October 1844 that Imam Shamil gave orders that every man who possessed a cow and pair of bullocks—that is, all except the very poor—should also provide himself with a horse. This seemed to point to an invasion of the Kumyk plain and valley of the Terek, but at the same time Keebat Mohoma and Haji Murad were ordered to assemble their guerrilla forces at Tiliti and Karata respectively. Thus all points were threatened, and Gourko was very much worried. Finally, he arrived at the conclusion that the danger was greatest in the north, and on 22 October left Shura, and by well concerted movements with Freitag, commanding the left flank, secured it.

Imam Shamil meant to strike only if it could be done without too great a risk, but was quite satisfied with his success in drawing Gourko away from Shura, and thereby ensuring the capture of Gherghebil, and eventually of Khounzakh. Acting on interior lines against an enemy not strong enough to guard himself at all points, he was sure of being able to strike with success somewhere; and, once more, his strategy was fully justified by the event. On 30 October Gourko, satisfied that the danger to the north had been averted, returned to Shura, but on the way learnt that Gherghebil was beleaguered by Keebat Mohoma two days ago. He gathered all his available forces—some 1,600 bayonets—and marched to the rescue; but on 6 November, when in sight of the fort, which lay below him a commander's council of war, decided that the task was

.

impossible, and he retired to Shura, leaving the garrison to its fate. The worst part of it was that the Russians in the fort were abandoned after they were sure of the outside help. Although these defenders were bitterly disappointed still they fought till their last.

No sooner did Gherghebil fall, Gourko sent orders to Passek to evacuate Khounzakh, but the message only reached him on 11 November and for the time its compliance was impossible. Tanous and Irganai were occupied in force by the mujahidin.

On the 16th, when Gourko found that Haji Murad had gone to join Imam Shamil, he hastily made his preparations in great secrecy, and managed to reach Ziriani safely along with the sick and wounded as well as all ammunition. Here he was immediately surrounded, and had to suffer at the hands of the mujahidin for an entire month.

Meanwhile on 9 November 1844 the mujahidin had destroyed a guard of fifteen men near Tarkou and appeared in the neighbourhood of Shura. Next day the garrison at Ghimry was vacated by the Russians. On the 11th Imam Shamil in person appeared at Kazanishchi, ten miles from Shura, and, taking possession of the village on all sides, blockaded Gourko in his capital. The eight-day siege of Neezovoe had then already begun, and Fort Evgenievskoe was also surrounded, so that on the 17th when the Khounzakh force was blocked at Ziriani, every Russian soldier in northern Daghestan was shut up within the entrenchments at one or other of these four places.

It was a real brilliant move of the Imam and proved his superior military genius. Had it not been for the reinforcements of General Freitag there was hardly any hope of the survival of a single Russian soldier. Even, then, since 27 August the Russians lost 92 officers and 2,538 men besides twelve fortified places and 27 guns.

The martyrdom of Akhverda Mohoma

Imam Shamil achieved unprecedented success this year. There was however, a sad incident and that is the death of his favourite lieutenant, Akhverda Mohoma, *naib* of little Chechnya, a leader only slightly less valour than Haji Murad. At the head of a force numbering some thousands Akhverda had marched against Shatil, the Khevsour stronghold on the upper waters of the Chanti Argun. The place was bravely defended by the Russians, and on the third day of the siege, the great Murid leader fell martyr to the cause for which he had lived a life full of dangers. He was one of the zealous and closest men to the Imam and it was a great loss for the movement.

A strange incident

The conditions of jihad wearied those who lacked faith in Allah. A few amongst such people drew up the evil design of submitting before the Russian government. However, they knew that any such compromise without the Imam's permission would prove to be fatal for these people. They tried to persuade Imam Shamil's mother, a respectable old woman renowned for her piety and goodness of heart. Being very tender hearted, she was greatly affected by the stories of Russian oppression and decided to ask favour from his son.

That very evening the old lady paid a visit to Imam Shamil, and after a long interview in private, came out, her eyes red with tears. What had passed between mother and son can only be guessed. What Imam Shamil did in the matter is related as follows.

Instead of punishing the four deputies of Chechens, who had begged favour through his mother, he announced his intention of retiring to fast and pray until such time as he could find his heart convinced on the right decision. Accordingly he shut himself up in the mosque, round which, at his command, the Murids and inhabitants of Dargo collected that they might join him in prayers. Three days and nights the door remained closed, and the mujahidin prayed along with their Imam. At last Imam Shamil appeared before his people, pale, exhausted, with bloodshot eyes, as from much weeping. Accompanied by two of his Murids he silently ascended the flat roof of the mosque, and at his command his mother was brought there, wrapped in a white shawl. Led by two mullahs, with slow, uncertain steps, she approached her son, who for some minutes gazed upon her without speaking. Then, raising his eyes to heaven, he exclaimed:

Sacred and unchangeable are Thy commands! Let Thy just sentence be fulfilled as an example to all the believers!

Then, turning to the people, he explained that the Chechens, unmindful of their oath of jihad had determined to submit to the giaour, and had sent deputies who, not daring to come directly to him, had addressed themselves to his mother, hoping to secure her intervention in this affair.

Her insistence and my boundless devotion to her inspired me with boldness to inquire at the will of Allah, and lo! here in your presence, aided by your prayers, I have after three days of prayer and fasting obtained the grace of his answer. But this answer has smitten me as would a thunderbolt. It is the will of Allah that whoever first transmitted to me the shameful intentions of the Chechen people should receive one hundred severe blows, and that person is my own mother!

Then at the Imam's command the Murids were asked to execute the punishment. At the fifth blow the victim fainted, and Imam Shamil moved beyond endurance, stayed the hands of the executioners and threw himself at his mother's feet. With tears and groans they implored mercy for their benefactress; and Imam Shamil, rising after a few moments without a trace of his former emotion, once more raised his eyes to heaven, and in a solemn voice exclaimed, "There is no God but the one God, and Muhammad is His Prophet! O dwellers in Paradise, ye have heard my heartfelt prayer, and have allowed me to take upon myself the remaining strokes that were allotted to my poor mother. These blows I accept with joy as a priceless gift." And with a smile on his lips took off his red robe, armed the two Murids with thick *nogai*[5] whips, and assuring them that he would kill with his own hand him who dared to trifle with the will of Allah and his Prophet, silently, and without betraying the least sign of suffering received the ninety-five remaining blows. Then, resuming his outer garments and coming down from the

---

5. A short, thick whip with round cross-section used by Cossacks of Russia, borrowed from Nogai people (an ethnic group of Daghestan).

roof of the mosque, Shamil strode into the midst of the awestruck crowd and asked, "Where are those villains through whom my mother has suffered so shameful a punishment?" The trembling deputies were instantly dragged forth and hurled at his feet, no one doubting their fate. But to their amazement and that of the silent, breathless crowd, instead of the severest punishment all expected, the Imam told them "Go back to your people, and in reply to their foolish demand tell them all you have seen and heard."

Nicolay's letter

In his comfortable palace in St. Petersburg, Emperor Nicolay could hardly visualise the difficulties his general had to face. He ordered General Neidhardt to enter the mountains and "defeat and scatter all Shamil's hordes, destroy all his military institutions, take possession of all the most important points in the mountains, and fortify those the retention of which may seem necessary". For this purpose he ordered the army of the Caucasus to be reinforced immediately by 26 battalions, including sappers, four regiments of Cossacks, and forty guns from Russia, besides filling up the ranks already on the spot by 22,000 experienced men and properly drilled recruits.

"As to your plan of action, the war minister will give you full instructions; these and the forces I assign for the attainment of the desired end. It will be for you to accept these views wholly or in part, but remembering always that, (1) from such gigantic means I expect corresponding results; (2) the operations must be decisive and straight to the point, with no diversion to any side issues; (3) in no case have I any intention of leaving the reinforcements now entrusted to you in the Caucasus beyond the month of December 1844."

The emperor also suggested that regardless of expense, some of Imam Shamil's supporters, particularly his former teacher (and father-in-law) Jamaluddin, the *qadis* of Akhousha and Tsoudakhar, and Keebat Mohoma of Tiliti should be bribed. Dissensions and disagreements would be spread amongst the rest of those nearest to the Imam, and, finally, the tribes should be pacified. The proclamations were also to be distributed, to the effect that nothing whatever was intended against the religion, property or customs of the natives.

The British had also used similar tactics during the Ambela War in 1863, when they had written to various tribes of Buner[6] that their aim was to destroy the stronghold of mujahidin at Malka and they would in no way interfere in the religion or customs of the tribes.[7] Imam Shamil's success in 1843 had not been confined to the scene of his military operations. Kaitago and Tabassaran districts facing the Caspian Sea had also revolted against the Russians. Southward the anti-Russian movement spread over the Kazi-Kumyks, as well as the Jaro communities, and inspired the neighbouring Muslim provinces. To the north even the peaceable Kumyks became restless, and warlike Kabarda, west of Vladikavkaz, showed great enthusiasm for jihad. The

6. Situated close to the borders of Afghanistan.

7. W. H. Paget and A. H. Mason, *Expeditions versus the North West Frontier Tribes* (London, 1884).

message of the Imam had spread through the entire Caucasus and he had attained the position of the central figure against Russian imperialistic designs.

Imam Shamil's defence plan was devised in such a masterly way that the Russian General Luders, who was in command at Avar Koisu, did not venture to attack Avaria in July 1844 and another attempt made by Argutinsky-Dolgorukov on Keebat Mohoma's stronghold, Tiliti, also failed. In Chechnya as elsewhere, there was a good deal of irregular warfare, in which the Russians had experience in actual fighting, but there were no encounters of serious importance, and Imam Shamil continued to enhance his popularity and hold over large parts of Caucasus. The popularity of the cause of jihad was such that Daniel, Sultan of Elisou, an influential native ruler, and a major general in the Russian service, decided to side with the Imam and secured to Shamil for many years to come the loyalty of whole districts in south Daghestan.

7

The Unsuccessful
Dargo Expedition

Disappointed with the meagre results obtained in 1844, Emperor Nicolay, an autocrat who never tolerated any disagreement with him, drew new plans to conquer the mountains which he could not subdue earlier.

To ensure the success of these plans General Neidhardt was replaced by Count Vorontsov, an aristocrat and a brilliant commander in the Napoleonic war. He was entrusted with the chief command in the field, and was also made viceroy of the Caucasus. Equipping the force of Caucasus with the best armoury he expected corresponding results and explicitly told that the fighting corps would have to return by the end of the year from Caucasus.

The new commander-in-chief, fresh from the council chamber in St. Petersburg, and pledged to carry out the emperor's wishes, overruled the objections of the local generals over the planning of St. Petersburg, as indeed they had already been overruled by his predecessor. However, within a short time, he had himself instilled some doubts into his mind as to the prospects of success. On 25 May he wrote to the war minister: "If, even the orders I received to take the offensive this year, before resuming the construction of the Chechen advanced line, were at variance with my own opinion, as they are with those of all the local generals, I should still carry them out with the same zeal: but I tell every one here frankly that it is not so, and that it seems to me unwise to avoid meeting Shamil and doing him harm if possible, which would help us more than anything else. If God is not pleased to bless us with success we shall nevertheless have done our duty, we shall not be to blame, and we can then turn, somewhat later, to the methodical system which will bear fruit, though of course not so quickly as a victory over Shamil himself."

When the leader of an expedition talks of possible failure, and all his chief subordinates anticipate it, the chances of success can best be judged. The truth of the matter is that those at St. Petersburg had hardly any knowledge about the real prowess of Imam and his forces. They dismissed him as a mere leader of a gang of people and thought that more resources and more number of troops would bring Imam to his knees. It was however without precedence in history, and the Tsars boasted so much of his military might and unbounded sources that they simply ruled out defeat. Depending on the contours of the maps and plans of the war council, they had hardly any clue of the difficult conditions which the Russian troops actually had to face.

Many times they would assign such missions to their commanders which would prove suicidal. The commanders were forced to execute them and they could not budge an inch from their orders. Even Count Vorontsov could write to his war minister in these words, "I dare not hope much success from our enterprise, but I will do all I can, of course, to carry out the emperor's desire and justify his confidence."

Next day he set out from Vnezapnaya with the Chechnya column, and was joined by the Daghestan column, the total force being no less than 18,000 strong, including twelve infantry battalions, two companies of engineers, 83 Cossack companies, 1,000 local militia and 28 generals. Daghestan column had nine Battalions, two companies of engineers, two companies of marksmen, eight cavalry regiments and eighteen guns. Never before had such a large army attacked Daghestan and Chechnya.

The military genius of Imam Shamil
Imam Shamil, as usual, based his strategy on a complete and masterly appreciation of all the conditions affecting both himself and his enemy. He knew that, as Argutinsky had pointed out, the Russians in present circumstances could penetrate the mountains but could not maintain themselves there. He also knew that he had no earthly chance of beating such an army as this in the open, nor even of harassing it seriously on the outward march, while men and horses were fresh, ammunition plentiful, and supplies adequate. His opportunity would come later on when the Russian invaders, worn with toil and weak from hunger, would have to face the homeward march over the barren mountains of Daghestan

or through the forests of Ichkeria. Then indeed he would let loose on them his mobile hordes like the wrath of Allah, break down the roads in front of them, seize every opportunity of cutting off front or rear guard, of throwing the centre with its weary baggage train and lengthy line of wounded into confusion, and give the men no rest by day or by night. At best they could succeed in fighting their way back to their base on the Soulak or Sundja, but he would take care that it should be in such plight as would lower them in their own eyes and in the eyes of every native from the Caspian to the Black Sea, from Terek to the Persian frontier.

Meantime he would show just enough force to lure them on, and if, with the help of Allah he succeeded in enticing them to his forest stronghold, Dargo, there was a chance at least of his serving Vorontsov as Grabbe had been served in 1842. The Russian did fall into the trap prepared masterly by the supreme tactician.

The Russian advance
The Russian columns, having united on 3 June 1845 and resumed their march the same day, and crossing the Terengoul which had defied an expedition sent against it the previous year, took possession of Old Burtunai, without resistance, to the disappointment of those who had hoped that they could achieve a victory here over the forces of the Imam.

On 5 June a reconnaissance in force of the Kirk Pass (8,070 feet), between Salatau Gumbet, developed into a forward movement of the whole army. The pass was undefended, and the Russian advance guard under Passek went down the other side to the abandoned fort Udachnaya, built by Grabbe on his way to Arguani and Akhulgo in 1839, and stormed the opposite height, Antchimeer (7,396 feet), in the face of a half-hearted opposition from a force of the mujahidin estimated at 3,000, with one gun.

Vorontsov described this affair in his report as one of the most brilliant he had ever witnessed, and it was undoubtedly a daring fact to attack so strong a position in the face of not much inferior numbers (Passek had had battalions, besides cavalry and artillery), but as the Russian loss in these circumstances was only 17 wounded, it is quite evident that the mujahidin had no plans to fight here. Now came the first blunder of the campaign, resulting in serious loss. On the morning of 6 June, Passek continued his advance without waiting for instruction, to the Zounon-Meer, ten miles farther on. Here he was for some time practically isolated; the weather changed suddenly from the summer heat to the severest cold, and for five days the unhappy troops, in wind, frost, and snow, and without provisions, suffered terribly. No less than 450 were frost-bitten, and 500 horses died.

The Imam's strategy
Leaving large forces to guard his communications, Vorontsov joined Passek on 11 June, and on the 12th took up ground near the aoul of Tiliti in sight of the Andy gates or gap, a strong position which, according to spies, Imam Shamil meant to defend to the last. Next day orders were given for the assault, but again the invaders were disappointed. The gates were undefended, though walled up

and flanked by breastworks. Imam Shamil had prepared to hold them when still uncertain what force would be brought against him, but seeing how strong the enemy was in artillery, he was much too wise to allow certain failure. He retired and set fire to Andy and the surrounding aouls, so that the Russians could not take any provisions from there.

On 14 June the Russians took possession of the ruins of Gagatl and Andy, driving out a small number of mountaineers. On the terraced slope of the mountain called Aval, Imam Shamil had taken his stand with some 6,000 men and three guns, hoping to harass the enemy down below, and Bariatinsky, with two companies of the Kabarda regiment and the Georgian and other native troops following, was for a time in a position of some danger.

Reinforcements, however, arrived, the mountain was taken, and Imam Shamil retired successfully without any harm done to his forces. The emperor wrote in a letter "Thank God, Who had made the Russian soldiers victorious. I am sure you will destroy Shamil's influence."

It was already evident to Vorontsov that there could be no question of establishing Russian authority so far away from his base. On 17 June he wrote, "It is evident that if ever we are to establish ourselves firmly in Andy, it is not from Chirkei or Vnezapnaya that we can draw our supplies, a proceeding nearly impossible in summer, and quite out of the question during the rest of the year."

Argutinsky and Freitag were right; at best the columns would return without having accomplished any permanent result; it would be well if they returned without serious loss. Already the difficulty of supplying the army was making itself felt, and during the first four days at Andy the men were on very short rations, though more than a third of the expeditionary corps had been left behind on the lines of communication, and Prince Beboutov, commander of the Daghestan column, had been specially detailed to hurry forward the convoys. It would have been better to recognise the force of circumstances and retreat before matters grew worse; but with Dargo only ten miles away, it is not to be wondered at that Vorontsov, with an experienced army of 10,000 men still available for the purpose, should have remained determined to attack Imam Shamil in his stronghold.

The word brilliant is not out of place as no Russian force in the Caucasus could compare with this in outward lusture, in all that goes to make up the "pomp and the glorious war".

The splendour of the Russian forces

Count Vorontsov's name and fame had attracted round him a galaxy of aristocrats from St. Petersburg and Moscow anxious to serve under so renowned a commander, and take part with him in the anticipated defeat of Imam Shamil and final conquest of the Caucasus. His staff and suite included Prince Alexander, Prince Wittgenstein, the Prince of Warsaw, and many aristocrats; his personal convoy a band of Kurds in picturesque national costume.

Then General Luders, commander of the 5th Army Corps, Klugenau, Passek, and others had each a numerous staff, and to distinguish their position in the camp or field each general had a penon fastened to a lance—the commander-in-chief, red and white with a horsetail tufts;

Luders, red-black, white with a silver cross; and so on. The number of non-combatants—boy servants, grooms, cooks, and companies—was naturally large; and the amount of camp furniture, officers' stores, horses and tents out of all proportion to the fighting forces—at least according to local ideas.

It seemed as if they had come to attend a coronation ceremony rather than a battle in the Caucasus. The men of the permanent regiments of the Caucasus—though Mourviov, Vorontsov's successors, stigmatised them as 'luxurious' until they won him victories and fame—looked down on the battalions from Russia, and with great contempt on the pampered menials of the staff officers. The latter, with their smart uniforms, dandy manners and complete ignorance of Caucasian or any other warfare, were little to the taste of the local officers, soldiers and nothing more; and, in turn, felt little sympathy, though they spoke pure Russian instead of beginning every sentence with a fashionable French phrases. They wore uniforms made by the regimental tailor, had nonetheless, fought many a desperate action. The army from St. Petersburg could hardly face the dynamic guerrillas of Imam Shamil. When it came to fighting, the local battalions had to bear the brunt of the struggle.

The provision trains came in slowly, and brought so little that it was impossible to accumulate more than a few days' rations, though Vorontsov waited three weeks in Andy for it. As far as local supplies, were concerned the army might as well have been in the middle of the Sahara. Imam Shamil knew his job, and had taken or destroyed everything eatable

by human beings for miles round. The sun had done the
rest, for the grass was burnt up, leaving the horses worse off
than the men. Local population might have helped the
Russians but the Imam had also catered for it. A Russian
officer during one of his patrols saw two human heads on
which this sentence was written in the Tartar language:
"Such is the fate of those who help the Russians."

On 18 June a considerable force was sent in the direction
of Botlikh, and bivouacked near the lake Ardjiam; but it
returned, having accomplished nothing but the destruction
of a few dozen trout, and was named the "trout expedition".

The march on Dargo

On 4 July, finding that he had but a few days' rations and
that the next convoy could not arrive before the 10th, so
that he would be no better off in this respect and would have
wasted another week, Vorontsov made arrangements to start
for Dargo on the morning of the 6th, with the intention of
sending back part of his force to take the provisions when
they arrived. It was a decision which the Russians were to
repent later on.

At 3.00 am on 6 June, Imam Shamil's spy, who was
serving in disguise in attendance on Count Vorontsov, took
his favourite horse and galloped off to warn the Imam that
the Russians were about to start. An hour later the march
began, and by 9.00 the whole of the troops had reached the
edge of the forest. Here a few hours' halt was called, while
the men rested and ate their dinner before the attack.

A beautiful scene extended towards the north. River
Terek looked like a silvery line and on the other side of it

was Russian border. Many soldiers were to see this scene for the last time in their lives. The road to Dargo was not more than four or five miles. But the track passed through a dense jungle. The track narrowed down at places to an extent that the force had to march in single column. There were huge trees on both sides and their branches had mingled. More so the guerrilla bands of the mujahidin were in waiting for the Russian army to cross this difficult path.

Russian advance

Towards 1.00 pm, General Luders, who had begged permission for the Litovsky regiment to lead the attack addressed them in a few stirring phrases. The men brandished their muskets above their heads, and vowed they would prove their mettle in the battlefield. The moment the advance was sounded, headed by their own officers and many of the staff, they rushed forward and surmounted one after the other the first six barriers, meeting with not very strong opposition, and suffering little loss. Behind them came the sappers to clear the way for the rest of the column. The speed of the advance just suited the tactics of the Imam's guerrillas who were ever on the look out to separate the enemy's column and endeavour to destroy it in detail.

When the commander-in-chief, riding quietly along with General Luders, followed by his staff and Prince Alexander, reached the narrow neck between the second and third obstacles, he was met by a heavy fire of musketry, and for a time was in imminent danger. The van by this time was far ahead, and the intervening space re-occupied by the enemy. All stopped; as many as forty officers were crowded together exposed to heavy fire. A mountain gun was sent for, and on arrival turned sideways to sweep the wooded ravine on the right flank from where the shots were coming, but after the second discharge every man serving it was killed or badly wounded. It was manned again, and in a few minutes the result was the same. For a brief space of time the gun was alone but for the dead and dying round it; no one dared to cross the neck. Then an ensign ran forward; an officer followed and came back unharmed but the piece was not served.

At this juncture General Fok made his way to the gun and loaded it himself, but before he could fire it, fell mortally wounded. Vorontsov then sent some Georgian militia and dismounted Cossacks into the wood, after which the shots stopped.

Meantime the Kabarda battalion which had followed the Litovsky men came up with them at the sixth obstacle, and the latter then continued their victorious onset till they reached an elevated space of open ground and saw Dargo far below them, about a mile distant. Here they halted until Vorontsov arrived, late in the evening, and ordered Bieliavsky, in command of the advance guard, to take possession of the aoul, which by that time was in flames, destroyed by Imam Shamil himself.

At 2.00 pm, the commander-in-chief reached Dargo and bivouacked for the whole of the troops came in. The losses were not great, though greater than need be: one general, three other officers, and 32 men killed; nine officers and 160 men wounded.

The Imam's capital was taken; but he had given no

opportunity of inflicting any serious loss. It was impossible to remain at Dargo, and the army had before it 28 miles of forest, every yard of which presented enormous difficulties. Grabbe in 1842 with the same strength had suffered defeat and disaster in retreating about half the distance to Gherzel aoul with only 2,000 men against him.

Imam Shamil with all his men were at hand, bent on the destruction of Russian force. The situation, foreseen by the veterans of Caucasian warfare, was in any case one of very great danger; the mistakes that were about to be committed rendered disaster inevitable.

The provisions could survive for another five days, and undoubtedly it would have been wisest to push on to Gherzel aoul as fast as possible, sending orders to the commanders in Daghestan to retire on the Soulak. But Vorontsov decided to keep to his plan and wait the arrival of the expected convoy.

Much interest was excited, meantime, by that part of Dargo which had been inhabited by the Russian deserters. The feelings of the Russian army may be imagined when at sunset these 600 soldiers marched to and fro on the left bank of the Aksai playing the Russian tattoo. This was the unkindest cut of all. On the same height Imam Shamil placed four guns which kept on pounding the Russian positions. An army attacked the position of the mujahidin on the morning of 8 July under General Labeentsev.

The attack was carried out and it seemed successful. The Imam's forces disappeared, and the Russians, watching from the camp from below, were happy, but at the time of retreat their joy was turned to grief. The way lay through fields of maize, where it was difficult to keep order or touch. On either side there was broken, wooded ground, and from behind each tree and stone, sprung up at once the guerrilla fighters.

The Russian soldiers dropped on all sides; the column returned to camp with a loss of 187 killed and wounded; the forces of the Imam re-occupied their former position, and morning and evening the Russian deserters played tattoo.

The moment the column began to retire was the turning point of the whole campaign. An inexplicable depression pervaded the whole army. The Russian soldiers who a few minutes before had been cheerful became serious and sad. It was not the sight of nearly 200 killed and wounded, but the conviction that the Russian sacrifice had been in vain.

The continuous chanting of the funeral service by the Orthodox priests, and volley firing as the bodies were lowered into their graves, deepened the general feeling of depression, and informed Imam Shamil about the number of the killed. Moreover, powder was already in short supply. The Russians now started burying their dead in silence.

On the evening of 9 July, rockets sent up from the edge of the forest, where the troops had rested on the 6th, told that the convoy had arrived. Obviously it could not reach Dargo unaided and the unhappy enterprise known ever since as the "Biscuit expedition" was organised.

The provisions being for all units alike it was decided that each should send half its strength to bring in its own share. Thus the column which was entrusted to Klugenau, with Passek in command of the advanced guard, Victorov of the rear, and amounted properly to some 4,000 men, was about as heterogeneous a force as could well be imagined.

The column started on the morning of the 10th to cover the four to five miles of pathway already described, along which every barrier destroyed with so much toil on the 6th had meanwhile been rebuilt more strongly than before, and some others were also added. Passek with two battalions of the Kabarda regiment, a company each of sappers and sharpshooters, and two mountain guns, dashed on ahead, storming one barrier after another, and Klugenau went with him. Naturally the centre became separated from the van, the rear from the centre and the guerrilla forces of the Imam swarmed in between, firing from every point of vantage, from behind every tree trunk, even from the branches overhead. As in Grabbe's expedition, the giant beech tree gave shelter to numerous Chechen sharpshooters and wherever confusion ensued, rushed in to complete the work with sword and *kindjal*.

The narrow ridge was the scene of confused and desperate fighting the entire summer's day, and only at nightfall, with the help of the vanguard sent back for the purpose did the remains of the column reach the open. General Victorov, General Fok and many officers and men had been killed, large numbers wounded and two guns lost.

The position was now a deplorable one, but worse was still to follow. Klugenau rightly thought that it would be better to make his retreat through Daghestan, leaving Vorontsov to fight his way with his remaining forces to Gherzel auol, rather than risk for the third time the passage of that terrible ride, encumbered as he now was with the supplies and the wounded (faced, too, by a triumphant enemy). A messenger was found daring enough to carry a second letter to Vorontsov, telling him that the column would start on its return to camp at dawn, and we can judge how falsely that commander-in-chief viewed the situation from the fact that he received the messenger with joy, and promoted him on the spot.

On the morning of 11 July the convoy started. Three cannon shots gave notice to those at Dargo that it was in movement, and soon the line of smoke above the trees showed where it fought its way down the bloodstained ridge. The mujahidin were in greater numbers than before; the barriers had once more been renewed, and a heavy rainfall had added greatly to the difficulties of the march. Passek again commanded the advance guard, and fought his way to the narrow neck already mentioned. Here he found a breastwork of trees faced with the Russian dead of the day before, piled one on top of the other. There were no defenders behind this ghastly obstacle, but it was enfiladed from smaller breastworks on either side, and until these were taken, no progress was possible. Men were falling every moment, and already the column was in confusion. Passek sent two companies of the Lioublin regiment against the right hand breastwork under Valkhovsky, a young guardsman, who led them gallantly, and was the first to surmount the obstacle, but fell dead the moment after. The companies lost many men and fell back in disorder.

Meantime Passek himself led the two remaining companies of the same regiment against the left-hand work. Passek was killed, and in such plight that no one was near him. It was a great shame for the Russian army to let their commander die such a helpless and miserable death. Although individual officers and men displayed great bravery, the stigma on the Russian army remained unwashed.

The sappers, meantime, certain that the position had been won, went to work to clear their way through the main barrier, but were overwhelmed and cut to pieces. They were followed by the straggling line, composed of details of all regiments and of all arms, encumbered with the heavy load of biscuits and an ever increasing number of wounded. Somehow or other with Klugenau's help, who led companies to the attack like any ordinary captain, they struggled to come out of the ridge step by step, fighting throughout, in groups, in handfuls, by ones, twos and threes. The guerrilla fire never ceased, and from time to time the mujahidin boldly dashed right into the Russian line.

The plight of the Russians was miserable but luckily enough for them, they had realised, though late, what was happening, and had sent off one battalion to the rescue, followed by other detachments who forced their way through and managed to reach camp late at night with all their wounded men.

The losses of 10–11 July were two generals, 17 officers and 537 men killed, 32 officers and 738 men wounded, three guns lost. Of the provisions for which all this sacrifice was made, hardly any reached Dargo. Vorontsoff, with a force reduced to 5,000 bayonets, burdened with the care of over 1,100 wounded with little or nothing to eat, and surrounded by the victorious guerrilla fighters, had still to cut his way through the 41 miles of forest that separated him

from Gherzel aoul. It was a hopeless task, and he knew it.
On its own the column could hardly win through by any
possibility. As with Shura in 1843, there was only one chance of
salvation. Freitag was at Grozny, and could have come to
their rescue. Five separate messengers were sent speeding
through the forest to warn the commander of the left flank
that his chief was desperately marching on Gherzel aoul,
and that it could escape total disaster only by his hurrying to
that place with all the troops he could manage. If the
message got through, there was still hope. Otherwise, not a
man could reach the plain alive.

Vorontsov had written to Freitag somewhat earlier asking
his opinion as to the proposed march on Gharzel aoul, to
which the commander of the left flank replied on 5 July:

> Amongst the Chechens it is already no secret that Your
> Excellency intends to come down to the plains from Dargo.
> 'We have not yet begun to fight the Russians,' they say. 'Let
> them go where they will, we know where to attack them.' And
> indeed they do know in the forests all advantages are on their
> side, and they understand well how to make the most of them.
> Your Excellency has given me permission to express my
> opinion. I cannot justify such flattering confidence better than
> by being absolutely frank. On the downward march you will
> meet in the forest such difficulties and such opposition as,
> probably, you do not anticipate. I will not attempt to prove
> that the operation is well-nigh impossible; on the contrary, I
> feel sure that Your Excellency will win through: but the losses
> will be enormous. You will find that the Chechens are
> experienced warriors.

Freitag went on to advise that formation on the march

called "carrying the column in a box" as the best in forest
fighting, and continues:

> I promised to be frank, and frank I must be. Judging from
> Your Excellency's letter, you seem to expect important results
> from the march through the forest to the plain. Allow me to
> say, simply, you are being deceived. However successful your
> movements, they will have no influence on the subjugation...
> From the fears I have expressed you may feel assured that I
> view your march far too seriously to allow of my remaining
> quiet, and I will do all I can not to have to blush for the
> confidence you have shown me. I hope to receive news when
> you start from my spies, but it is desirable that I should be
> informed in good time.

The Russian plight

The next few days brought all the misery which the guerrilla
forces of the Imam were capable of inflicting on the enemy.
The Russians spent the 12th of July in preparations for the
march, including arrangements for the transport of the
wounded, and destroying all tents and such stores as were
not absolutely necessary.

On 13 July a start was made at dawn. There was not much
fighting, but progress was terribly slow, and the column
stayed at Tsonteree for the night having progressed only
three miles. On the 14th, the march continued to Shouani,
where the road or path branched in one direction to
Mayortoup, in the other to Gherzel aoul. Here Imam Shamil
had determined to make his stand and bring matters to a
conclusion if possible, and it is said that his *naibs* had sworn
not to let the Russians pass this spot.

There was much hard fighting, but by evening the

column had won a position near Issa Yourt, on the left bank of the Aksai, opposite Sayasani, twelve miles from Tsenteree, and halted, having lost in the two days seven officers and 70 men, and added 24 officers and 225 men to its list of wounded.

The Russian vanguard had hurried on; Imam Shamil's guerrillas had taken advantage of the fact, and rushing on the centre, composed of the 5th Army Crops with their huge convoy of stores and wounded, had committed much havoc.

On 15 July the Russians exhausted by the previous day's fighting, were incapable of marching any further and though the guerrillas gave little trouble, Vorontsov halted at Alleropy, only four miles farther on. 15 men were killed, while three officers and 63 men wounded.

16 July was a disastrous day for the Russians as the guerrillas were determined and the Russians played into their hands, repeating, incredible as it may seem, the same mistake that has already cost so much blood and suffering. Throughout the campaign the Russian column had been committing the mistake of being divided into two. No sooner had the men surmounted one obstacle than they found another confronting them.

The way was along the thickly wooded left bank of the Aksai, up and down hill, in addition to which there were the usual barriers of felled or fallen trees at every convenient spot. The fighting was of the closest kind, often hand to hand; each step in advance led naturally to the next, besides which every soldier knew that the only chance of safety led in reaching Gherzel aoul or its neighbourhood within the next two or three days at most, and pressed on with feverish haste. The usual consequences ensued—the column became broken; and the former scenes were repeated. Sappers were cut to pieces because the troops, who had taken the barriers they were to clear a road through, had gone ahead, and the enemy had closed in after them; artillery left uncovered, and every man killed or wounded.

By evening the miserable worn-out column had dragged itself to the aoul of Shaukhal Berdee, a distance of about five miles, and stopped there as the soldiers were exhausted. On the fourth day the losses were two officers and 107 men killed, 15 officers and 401 men wounded, the total losses since leaving Dargo were over a thousand, and Gherzel aoul was still 15 miles away, that is, the column had covered only 26 miles in four days, or at the rate of a little over six miles a day.

There were now more than 2,000 wounded altogether, there were three sound men to lead, carry, or guard each sick or wounded through that terrible forest, and do all the scouting and fighting in the van, the rear, and on either flank. The provisions had also come to an end, the men were already suffering from hunger, and were rapidly becoming demoralised.

When Vorontsov saw that to march any farther was impossible, he decided to await the arrival of Freitag, not knowing, however, whether his message from Dargo had ever reached the general or not. The whole of 17 July was spent in this terrible uncertainty; the soldiers had nothing to eat but a small amount of maize. Small arms and ammunition had almost finished, and the artillery had hardly a round left to answer the guns from which Imam

Shamil bombarded the camp at intervals throughout the whole day. The army was now actually starving, and a day or two at most would have brought the end.

The situation was so bad that it is alleged that Vorontsov had determined, if no help was forthcoming that day, to abandon the wounded and cut his way through to Gherzel aoul. This allegation may be false but it was nonetheless current in the camp. It indicates the miserable situation in which the whole of Russian army at this front was reduced by the guerrilla freedom-fighters of the Imam. The might of Tsar was razed to the ground.

The sixth day since the column left Dargo (18 July) passed like its predecessor without a sign from Freitag. Hunger grew more intense. The guns were without ammunition; the troops had only fifty rounds left. Imam Shamil kept up his bombardment, the Murids and their followers attacked from every side and sniped the camp from every place of vantage. The actual loss was not large, but it kept all on the alert.

The evening fell and it seemed to be the last night for most of the Russians, when the cannon shots were heard. Later on it was known that all five separate messengers, three natives and two Russians, who had been sent off from Dargo to summon his aid, had reached their destination between 15 and 16 July. Freitag had foreseen something of the sort, and had already made his arrangements, keeping his available troops ready between Grozny and Gherzel aoul. He set out without a moment's delay, rode 120 miles in two days, gathering his forces on the way, and at 9.00 pm, on 16 July, his advanced guard arrived on a small open space in full view of the besieged camp.

Next day Vorontsov moved out to meet him, and on 20 July, the remaining expeditionary force was safe at Gherzel aoul.

Imam Shamil, content with the sound beating which he had given to the enemy, retired alongwith his guerrillas without much harm to his own force. Even on the final day of retreat the Russians lost three officers and 78 men, eight officers and 138 men were wounded. Freitag lost 14 men, one officer and 27 men wounded, while awaiting rescue.

In a long and interesting letter to Vorontsov, dated February 1846, Yermolov writes; "I do not dispute that if Freitag had not come by with fresh troops you would nonetheless have fought your way through. But how many of you?"

And he rightly corrects Vorontsov's statement that the Russians had never been at Dargo before, whereas Rosen and Valmeenov had been there in 1832.

The total losses of Vorontsov's army were three generals, 195 officers and 3,433 men—killed and wounded, alongside the loss of three guns.

Had it not been for the local battalions not a single man would have escaped. The battalion of the Doureen regiment, which had been used for flanking service, the most dangerous in forest warfare, lost 603 men and 23 officers out of 850, the Kabarda in the same proportion.

Thus the fateful Russian expedition which attempted to teach a lesson to Imam Shamil, was badly mauled due to the superior tactics of guerrilla warfare adopted by the Imam.

Che Guevara wrote the following in his *Guerrilla Warfare*

about a century after the Dargo campaign and it corresponds to the same strategy of the Imam in fighting the Russians:

> The guerrilla fighter knows the places where he fights. The invading column does not; the guerrilla fighter grows at night and the enemy feels his fear growing in the darkness. In this way without much difficulty, a column can be totally destroyed, or at least such losses can be inflicted upon it as to prevent its returning to battle and to force it to take a long time for regrouping.

> The defences and the whole defensive apparatus should be arranged in such a manner that the enemy vanguard will always fall into an ambush. As a psychological factor, it is very important that the men in the vanguard will die betrapped in every battle because this produces within the enemy army a growing consciousness of this danger until the moment arrives when nobody wants to be in the vanguard and it is obvious that a column with no vanguard cannot move, since somebody had to assume that responsibility.

8

Haji Murad

Dargo expedition had failed. On this occasion the only
excuse Vorontsov could offer the emperor for the heavy loss
sustained was that "the mountains have now learnt that we
can reach them in places hitherto deemed inaccessible". He
was determined in the future to advance systematically,
cautiously, and to seize only what could be held
permanently.

The Russians devoted the year 1846 mainly to
constructive work: the strengthening of existing forts and
fortresses, the addition of new ones, the improvement of
barrack accommodation, the building of a military road
from Akhtee into Georgia over the main chain and the
better coordination and dispositions of the various forces
constituting the army of the Caucasus.

The 5th Army Corps as such was to return to Russia,
leaving its second battalions as the nucleus of a whole new
division, to consist of four 5-battalion regiment of infantry
with a proportionate increase of artillery and engineers. No

offensive operations on a large scale were contemplated, and if any serious fighting took place it could only be as a result of hostile moves on Imam Shamil's part.

It is worth mentioning here that Major-General J.W. McQueen had offered same set of excuse when he wrote to the British government after the unsuccessful Black Mountain campaign.[1] He had written that the places so far inaccessible have been trampled under the British feet. The fact was ignored that the 'natives' had made their stay in those areas impossible. It seemed as if the Imam had prepared to strike at the territories of the Dargo confederacy. He was in fact secretly preparing for the invasion of Kabarda, the most unexpected of all his military enterprises.

This episode cannot be understood unless one knows about the freedom movement being waged by Western Caucasus against Russia. This movement kept aflame till 1864 and from time to time efforts were made to coordinate the armed resistance to Russia in both spheres of conflict. Emissaries were now and again despatched by the Cherkess and other tribes to seek aid or advice from Imam Shamil, who in turn sent his representatives amongst them to stir up movement of resistance when it was at low ebb, or to congratulate them on the success that from time to time crowned their efforts against the common enemy. Information as to what took place at any point, however

---

1. The Black Mountain campaign led by General John Withers McQueen in 1888 was to fight the tribes in the North West Frontier and bring them into submission to Britain.

distant, spread throughout the Caucasus so quick that it seems unbelievable in the absence of any advanced means of communication. Victory at one place would raise the morale of guerrilla fighters at other places. Thus destruction of the Russian fortresses on the Black Sea coast in 1840 was an important factor in Imam Shamil's recovery of power after Akhulgo.

The victory or the defeat of Russia had a great impact on the military potential of Russia and as such it was a matter of vital importance to Imam Shamil that fighting on the western front should continue. He decided that the time had come to extend the rule of *Shari'ah* from the Caspian Sea to the Black Sea.

In the east, from the neighbourhood of Vladikavkaz and the Georgian road almost to the Caspian, Muridism won a great success. In the west, from the upper waters of the Kuban to the Black Sea coast, the fight for independence continued. But in between lay Kabarda, inhabited by a warlike race related in blood to the Cherkess, which had accepted Russian rule, and since 1822 had abstained from open revolt, though of late increasingly restless. There was thus a gap in the very centre of the fighting line which unless cemented, must always separate the two main areas of conflict. If the Kabardans could take up arms, not only would east and west be linked together, but Imam Shamil's fighting strength would be greatly increased. Russia would then find herself face to face in the northern Caucasus with combined armies of freedom-fighters she had not yet come across.

Imam Shamil's great successes against the Russians

appealed to some of the leading princes who invited the Imam to come and join hands against Russia. The Imam was waiting for such an opportunity and at once decided to go accompanied by his Murids.

The gathering of the Murid hordes could not, of course, be kept secret. Owing to local conditions there were always too many spies in either camp to allow of any such secrecy. Every hostile movement was known to the opposing side almost as soon as initiated and its progress was watched and reported daily, even hourly. It has been mentioned earlier how the personal servant of Vorontsov had informed the Imam about the attack on Dargo beforehand. The Imam had an efficient intelligence organization.

The Russians who were holding exterior lines could seldom hope to conceal their designs. The concentration of their troops at any given point indicated quite clearly the object in view. The position of Imam Shamil was otherwise. Completely surrounded by hostile territory, and acting from within, he could gather his forces, and threaten the enemy in more directions than one, leaving them in doubt up to the last moment as to where the blow would fall. Having puzzled his enemy and completed his own preparation, he could choose where to strike in accordance with the defensive measures they had seen fit to adopt. On the present occasion he succeeded in convincing Argutinsky and Vorontsov himself that his chief aim was Akoush in central Daghestan and so satisfied was the Russian commander-in-chief on this head that remaining himself at Shemakha, in the south, he sent orders to Freitag expressly forbidding him to delay the homeward march of the army corps battalions.

It was early in April that Freitag, at Grozny, came to know of the Murid gathering in Chechnya where already during the month of March several daring attacks had been made on Russian troops. On 11 March, convinced already that the enemy had in view some enterprise of quite unusual scope and importance, he sent a message to General Hasfort at Mozdok requesting him—despite the positive orders received from St. Petersburg, and confirmed so recently by Vorontsov—not only to stay the homeward march of the two battalions, part of the 5th Army Corps already at that place, but to divert them to Nikolayevskaya, Cossack stanits on the Terek, thirty miles north-west of Vladikavkaz.

At this time Freitag had no positive knowledge of Imam Shamil's intentions, but this movement, together with the simultaneous retention of another battalion at Kizlyar, and the suitable disposal of his own command, provided as far as possible, in the circumstances, against all contingencies. For Nikolayevskaya covered, without actually guarding, the fort on the Terek opposite the minaret of Tatartoub, a strategic point of great importance already mentioned as the scene of Tamerlane's victory over Toktanuish and of Shaykh Mansur's defeat in 1785. If Imam Shamil intended to make any movement to the west of Vladikavkaz it was here that he must cross the Terek, and it is evident that Freitag's suspicion in this direction had already been roused. Vladikavkaz, itself was sufficiently garrisoned by 1300 men, and covered, moreover, by General Nesterov's small but compact force at Nazran. If, on the other hand, the Imam's objective was Kizlyar and the Kumyk plain, the additional battalion there would strengthen the local garrison very considerably. In either case Freitag's own little army of the left flank, being in a central position, could be concentrated at short notice ready to strike where needed. The contingency of a direct attack on himself was not, of course, worth consideration, and the other possibility, of a movement on Daghestan, was already provided for locally.

It was no light thing to disregard the commands of such a ruler as Nicolay I, who had only with the greatest reluctance allowed the 5th Army Corps to remain in the Caucasus beyond the term originally assigned, i.e. the end of 1844, and had now issued positive orders for its return. One must give due credit to this commander, who dared to disobey the orders of the Tsar in the best interests of his country.

Freitag's strategy was thoroughly sound, as events soon proved, but his position, nonetheless, was one of great anxiety. The information received left no doubt that Imam Shamil's levies would on this occasion outnumber by at least two to one the whole of the forces at his disposal, and being possessed of extraordinary mobility, could be hurled in overwhelming numbers on the units necessarily detached to the east or west of the Russian position. Freitag, it is true, would be on their heels within a few hours at most, but any start was a long one for such rapid movers as the Murids. The success of the Murid fighters was sure to have adverse effects on the morale of the Russians and would considerably boost the struggle for freedom.

Once more Imam Shamil was successful in his manoeuvers. Meller-Zokomelski had occupied, indeed, the wooded spur overlooking the river, but on Imam Shamil's approach, came down to meet him. The Imam saw the error, and profiting by it seized the position himself, and seconded by Haji Murad, rapidly passed the whole of his forces to the right bank with insignificant loss from Meller-Zokomelski's fire. The latter followed, and Freitag himself crossed the river in pursuit a few hours later.

But the great opportunity was lost. Imam Shamil and his guerrilla forces travelled considerably more than 67 miles in little over twenty-four hours, retracing at first the line of their outward march but, from the river Tsidakh, keeping right on for 60 miles through the barren valley between the Terek and Sundja ranges of hills. Crossing the latter opposite the Mikhailova and the Sundja itself near Kazakh-Kitchou on the morning of 27 March, they drove back into the fort the garrison of 400 men who had come out to intercept them, and from that moment were safe from pursuit.

Meller-Zokomelski pursued the Murids to beyond the Koupra, but not daring to face the desert space where even some of the locals had died of thirst, turned south through Achaluk, and at 7.00 pm on 27 March, reached the Sundja at Sundjenskaya. Nesterov's chance of intercepting the guerrillas had likewise been frustrated by the northerly route chosen for the retreat; and when Freitag, marching day and night, reached Kazakh-Kitchou at 8.00 pm on the same day, he was to find to his utter disappointment that the Imam had successfully out-manoeuvered him.

The treachery of the Kabardans
Although Imam Shamil could not fulfil his principal mission,

he had hardly suffered any material loss. He managed to save the entire strength of his forces by his successful movements. His reputation was enhanced by the fact that the Russians could not do any harm to him.

The fact that the Kabardans did not help the Imam in his campaign debased them in the eyes of other Caucasian tribes. Throughout the rest of the year, the guerrilla forces of the Imam remained active and gave the Russians no peace in either Daghestan or Chechnya. How daring were the attacks may be judged from the fact that they bombarded even Grozny and Vozdveezhenskoe.

In Daghestan, Haji Murad, while coming from Ghimry, raided the garrison of Shura and captured 158 horses and 188 head of cattle. He killed twenty men in this encounter.

The guerrilla fighters of the Imam were so active that in the course of this comparatively quiet year, the Russian army in Caucasus lost nearly 1,500 officers and men in killed, wounded and missing.

Preparation of defences

During the first three months of 1847 Imam Shamil lay quiet at Veden,[2] or Dargo-Veden, as he called it, in memory of the Dargo which had been destroyed two years earlier, and it appeared quite uncertain whether he would take the field or not. But on 28 March a brilliant meteor was seen there, and the same night the suburb or quarter occupied by the

---

2. Veden in the Chechen language means a flat place, and is applied to many of the small plateaus or flat-bottomed valleys in the mountains of Chechnya, generally with some distinguishing word before it, as Dishne-Veden, Benoi-Veden, Djano-Veden, etc.

Russian deserters was burnt to the ground. Shamil interpreted these events to his followers—firstly, as Allah's command to renew jihad, and secondly, as an indication of the fate in store for the infidels—and promptly put his forces in motion. Vorontsov, meantime, having learnt his lesson back in 1845, had been building forts and roads, instead of undertaking operations in the field.

During the first half of the year both sides made preparations. The Russian plans were comparatively modest, consisting mainly of the capture of Gherghebil, Saltee, Sogratl and Ireeb,[3] and the building of a fort at the first named aoul, to which Vorontsov attached great importance. From Imam Shamil's disposition for the defence of these places, it is quite evident that he was at this time, as usual, very well served by his spies and by his own knowledge.

The siege of Gherghebil

Gherghebil like other aouls already mentioned had a favourable defensive position, strong by nature and made stronger still by art. Rising in the form of an amphitheatre on the face of a hollow cone of rock at the foot of the Aimiakee defile, it was unapproachable on the north-west, where it overlooked a precipice, and on every other side was defended by fortified stone saklias, raising their tier to a kind of citadel in the middle. It was surrounded by a wall fourteen feet high and five feet thick. There were two flanking towers, each with a small cannon—the only artillery

---

3. Vorontsov to Tchernisheff, 13 February 1847: Akti, x. p. 442.

in the place—and the houses were loopholed in such manner that each tier might be swept by a crossfire from that above it. Within the aoul, wherever possible there were barricades, earthworks traverses, etc. All this was known to the Russians beforehand through their spies. The place was defended by a chosen hand sworn on the Qur'an to die rather than to yield—but one detail they did not know until the day of attack.

Prince Vorontsov reached Gherghebil on the 1st June, and took command of the united Daghestan and Samur divisions, numbering together ten battalions of infantry, besides a large miscellaneous force of cavalry, artillery and native levies. On 1 June, batteries were placed in position the same day and a heavy fire directed on the salient southern corner of the aoul, which seemed to promise the easiest entry. The next day the terraced gardens were taken without a shot being fired in their defence, owing, as was afterwards known, to the fact that cholera had broken out among the Murids. By the 3rd, a sufficient breach had been made, and Vorontsov, misled by feeble opposition into thinking that the garrison was weak, gave orders for the assault.

Meantime a significant event had occurred. On the heights above the left bank of the Kara Koisu, at an almost impregnable position, the mujahidin arrived in large numbers. Imam Shamil accompanied by his Murids had come in person to witness the final battle.

Russian attack
On the morning of 4 June, at 6.00, the Russian troops

attacked. Some columns, Yevdokimov, marched off at once. The duty assigned to it was to take up a position at the western side of the aoul, and at a given signal make a feigned attack in order to draw part of the garrison away from the point of assault. The storming column under Prince Orbeliani, consisting of the 21st battalion of the Apsheron regiment and one of the Princes of Warsaw's (Paskievich's), with a forlorn hope provided with ladders, and appeals with entrancing tools, was to make straight for the breach. Another battalion of Paskievich's and one of the Samur regiment were held in reserve; and Argutinsky-Dolgorukov's whole division was directed to keep watch on the enemy outside, and checkmate any attempt to aid the defenders. There was considerable delay, during which the batteries kept up a furious bombardment to widen the breach. In the intervals of the bombardment, the watchful Russians heard the melancholy long-drawn notes of the death-chant rising from behind the wall as from an open grave. More than ever convinced that he had to do with a mere handful of devoted brave warriors, Vorontsov at 9.00 in the morning ordered the signal rocket to be fired.

The Russians rushed forward, eventually scaling the wall far from the point intended, and suffered severely; the rest of the column kept the proper direction and the Apsheron men strove to mount the breach. Their comrades of the Warsaw regiment followed, but fire from hundreds of rifles moved the troops down like grass. Yevdokimov fell dead, pierced by a dozen bullets; Vinnikov, captain of the grenadier company, strode over his body and gained the top of the breach, but fell in the attack.

A Danish officer now led the troops forward, and the wall was won. The losses were already heavy but the Russians were determined. In front was the first row of low stone saklias, and, climbing their walls, the attackers rushed forward when to their horror the ground gave way beneath their feet, and amid shouts they fell on to the swords and *kindjals* of the Murids down below. The flat roofs had been taken off the whole of the lower row of houses, and replaced by layers of brushwood, thinly covered with earth. Every house in fact was a deathtrap, into which the unhappy stormers must fall, to be killed by the mujahidin. Some of their comrades saw and shuddered, but still the column came on, and soon nearly the whole of it was within the wall. Many officers, however, had fallen; the men, fighting their way into the aoul, singly or in small parties, became scattered and entangled amongst the houses or in the narrow streets, and no command was possible.

The Russians had to retreat, and rescuing with difficulty the wounded officers, the remnant of the column retreated through the breach. Here supported by the reserve, they formed up, and, mad with rage, demanded to be led forward once more. The second attempt was repetition of the first—the place was impregnable. The victorious Murids driving the broken columns a second time before them, followed until stopped by the bayonets of the reserve. In spite of the Russians' heroic bravery, the assault had failed, and the survivors returned to camp. The losses were great: 36 officers, and 851 men killed or wounded.

For four days more a pretense was made of maintaining the siege, but beyond keeping up a desultory artillery fire, nothing was done. Each night the enemy stole down from the hills and harassed the Russians till they were well-nigh worn out. Then cholera broke out, and Vorontsov, very much relieved of, abandoned his position and retired up the Kazi-Kumukh Koisu.[4]

Russian losses at Saltee

Vorontsov, now devoting his attention to Saltee, ordered vast quantities of siege material to be prepared by 1 July. After a regular siege of seven weeks, during which both sides displayed great heroism, Vorontsov took that aoul by storm at the third attempt. The Russian loss on this occasion amounted to 2,000, killed and wounded.[5]

In June of the following year (1848) he sent Argutinsky-Dolgorukov with 10,000 men back to Gherghebil, which the Murids this time abandoned by night after a twenty-three day siege, culminating in a terrific bombardment from forty-six guns of various calibre.[6] The Russian commander had on this occasion as his immediate assistants, destined like himself to become famous Wrangel and Orbeliani, brilliant and successful leaders; Yevdokimov and Bariatinsky, and Brimmer.

In the course of the siege the Russians fired 10,000 shells into this mountain village or against the Murids outside.

---

4. Vorontsov's report to Tchernisheff: Akti x. p. 450.

5. For Saltee, see Vorontsov's official report: Akti x. pp. 463-468. For the events of 1847 generally, Kavkazsy Sbornik, vi. pp. 477-482.

6. Arguteensky-Dolgorukov's reports: ibid; pp. 474 et seg.

Their losses were four officers and 76 men, and wounding 14 officers and 457 men. The mujahidin lost 1,000 mostly during the struggle that took place between Prince Bariatinsky and Haji Murad for possession of the orchards. The victors could hardly gain anything by their efforts, for they were not in a position to retain possession of Gherghebil, and retreated, closely pursued by the Murids, to Khodjal Makhee. The afterwards fortified Aimiakee at the other end of the chasm, which for many reasons was a better position, while Imam Shamil replaced Gherghebil by a strong fort, known as Ullu-Kala.[7]

The siege of Akhtee

In 1848, the Russians put a brave defence at Akhtee and it would be unfair not to mention the extraordinary valour displayed by the Russians in defending this fort on the Samur. Here, 500 men under Colonel Roth, and afterwards when he was wounded, under Captain Novoselov, held out for more than a week against many thousands under the command of Imam Shamil and his chief lieutenants, Daniel Sultan, Keebat Mohoma, and Haji Murad. Half the garrison was killed or wounded, the chief powder magazine blown up, the walls breached, water ran short, and no food could be cooked. Finally the Russians agreed to blow themselves up rather than fall into the hands of the enemy. As at Gherghebil in 1843, the defenders had the cruel experience of seeing a relieving force, under Argutinksy-Dolgoroukov, approach, but after vainly attempting to cross the Samur

---

7. *Kavkazsky Sbornik*, vii. pp. 483-538.

from the north, retired out of sight.

Some administrative reforms of Vorontsov

During the years 1848 to 1856, both the Russians and Imam Shamil stood on the defensive in Eastern Caucasus. There were comparatively few engagements of note, none involving very serious losses to either side. Imam Shamil was left in undisputed possession of western Daghestan, including Avaria, and of the greater part of Chechnya; but, on the other hand, the destruction of Saltee and Gherghebil, the building of forts at Aimiakee, Tsoudakhar and other places, and the establishment of permanent staff quarters with ample barrack accommodation at suitable strategic points, had greatly lessened the danger of invasion for Russia and the native states subject to her.

Prince Vorontsov, realising that he was not strong enough to deal Muridism a mortal blow under existing conditions, contented himself for the most part with strengthening his lines on all sides pending the advent of a favourable moment for resuming a more active policy, and otherwise devoted his very great abilities and energy to the reform of the civil administration. In this field, necessarily extensive and varied in a country like the Caucasus, he achieved enduring success, and on this his fame as viceroy of the Caucasus must rest. But his military aim was by no means one of merely passive defence, particular in Chechnya, where the ruthless partisan warfare went on as before, varied from time to time by raiding expeditions on a large scale.

Heroic deeds of Haji Murad

The Imam was busy building up his influence among the tribes as well as organizing them into one single formidable unit. Thousands of Murids had flocked under his banner and were ready to sacrifice their lives. Haji Murad, his prominent *naib*, could take them anywhere to teach a lesson to the Russians. The Russian successes at Saltee and Gherghebil in 1848, were balanced the following year, by the failure of Arguteensky's attempt on Keebat Mohoma's new fortress near Tchokh, occupying an unusually strong position even for Daghestan on a mountain some twelve miles south-east of Gunib. After a long bombardment, during which 22,000 shots and shells were fired at the place, the Russian commander retired rather than risk an assault, and Tchokh remained a virgin stronghold to the end of the war. Against this, in turn, the Russians could set the completion of the Akhtee military road, shortening communications between Tiflis and Shura by more than 250 miles, and remarkable, amongst other things, as comprising the first tunnel ever made in Russia.

Earlier in the same year (14 April) Haji Murad established his fame as the most daring of all the Murid leaders by a raid on Shura, the capital and chief military centre of Russian Daghestan, an event that called forth strictures from the emperor himself. It was on this occasion that he resorted to the well-known device of reversing the shoes of his horses to baffle those who pursued him.

The following year he made an incursion into eastern Georgia and put to the sword the whole Russian garrison at Babaratminskaya,

In 1851 Imam Shamil sent Haji Murad into the coastal provinces of Iaitago and Tabassaran to rouse once more the inhabitants against their Russian masters, and again he renowned himself by one of those daring escapades that have immortalised his fame in the annals of Caucasian warfare. With 500 horsemen he entered by night Nouinakh, a rich aoul on the military road between Derbent and Shura, killed Shakh Vali, brother of the Shamkhal of Tarkou, on his own threshold, and carried off captive his wife and children for whom Imam Shamil subsequently obtained a heavy ransom. On this occasion Haji Murad and his men rode 100 miles in less than thirty hours, and though hotly pursued, managed to escape. There were, indeed, no bounds to his daring, and it is not surprising that he became the terror of all those districts whose inhabitants had submitted to Russia, to such an extent that on one occasion 1,500 native militia under command of a Russian officer fled before a score or so of Murids who attacked them shouting "Haji Murad! Haji Murad!"

A misunderstanding

Haji Murad developed some misunderstanding with Imam Shamil and deserting his own forces, he gave himself up to the Russians. Haji Murad was led to believe that Imam Shamil wanted to get him killed as he was afraid of Murad's power. This was a great lie but Haji Murad misunderstood the Imam.

Colonel Prince Vorontsov sent him on to his father, the viceroy at Tiflis, who received him with joy, and obtained the emperor's consent to his remaining in the Caucasus, in

view of the services he might be expected to render; but
Nicolay, who wrote "Thank God, a good beginning" on the
margin of Vorontsov's letter announcing the surrender,
pointed out with characteristic distrust that a man who had
once turned traitor might do so again, and threw the whole
responsibility on Vorontsov.

Haji Murad was kept in a sort of honourable captivity at
Tiflis, but his family was at Tselmess, an area in which Imam
Shamil had strong hold. He was much disturbed because of
his forced separation from his family. He spent whole nights
in prayer and fell ill. He was sent, therefore, to Grozny to
see if he could manage their rescue. Failing in this, he
returned to Tiflis, and thence at his own request was sent to
Noukha, on the pretence that there he could observe more
strictly the rites of his faith.

Haji Murad now repented on whatever he had done. He
was now in the clutches of Ghayurs and was under strict
surveillance. He was also anxious to see his family. Like
Imam Shamil and other mujahidin, he was a very
affectionate father and a loving husband. He now decided to
flee and meet Imam Shamil to beg forgiveness.

One evening while riding with his four faithful followers
and escorted by only five or six Cossacks of the commander-
in-chief's convoy, Haji Murad suddenly drew a pistol, killed
the non-commissioned officer in command. One of his men
killed a Cossack, and the little party made off at full gallop.
Captain Boutehkeeyev, who was responsible for them,
hearing what had happened, quite lost his head and drove
straight off to Tiflis.

Vorontsov had undertaken a great personal

responsibility towards his stern master, and through the gross carelessness of his subordinate had now to face the unpleasant duty of informing Nicolay of Haji Murad's escape.

Luckily, however, for the Russians, the commandant at Noukha, Colonel Korganov, was a man of energy and judgement. Knowing that the defiles were guarded, he gave orders to the militia to follow the road to the plains taken by Haji Murad in 1850 in the raid on Babaratminskaya. Two days later, on 23 April 1852, Haji Murad was discovered and surrounded in a wood by a large party of militia, who were soon joined by other troops and by the inhabitants of the district led by a blood enemy of Haji Murad. And now took place one of those dramatic scenes so frequent in Caucasian warfare. Since escape was impossible, the Murids dug a pit with their *kindjals*, killed their horses, made of them a rampart and intoning their death-song,[8] prepared to kill as many of their enemies as possible. As long as their cartridges lasted they kept their enemies, a hundred to one, at bay; then Haji Murad, bare head, sword in hand, leapt up and rushed out to meet martyrdom along with two of his men. The other two were severely wounded and taken prisoners before being executed.

On 24 April 1852, Haji Murad died as he had lived—desperately brave. His ambition equaled his courage and to that there was no bound. He was a brave son of a brave nation. He enjoyed dangers and considered the uneasy and difficult life of the mountainous terrain better

---

8. See Appendix II.

than the comforts of slavish life in Russia. He considered honourable death better than a shameless life and lived up to this ideal through his blood.

General Okolnitichi says of Haji Murad: "He had not, like Shamil, the talent requisite for directing large and serious military undertakings; but, on the other hand, none ever excelled him in daring and enterprise as a leader of raiding parties. It was a light matter for him, with a party of 400 or 500 horsemen, to appear suddenly at the rear of our troops, far inside our own boundary; to ride fifty miles today, eighty tomorrow; draw off attention by false alarm, and profiting by the general panic, escape unhurt. These qualities obtained for Haji Murad, in the course of time, such renown in the mountains as no other *naib* enjoyed."[9]

Prince Bariatinsky

In 1852 Prince Bariatinsky became chief of the left Flank and had a force of 10,000 made under his command. A year later Bariatinsky came to the Caucasus as viceroy and commander-in-chief. He considered all the flaws of previous campaigns and drew newer and bolder plans. Some progress had already been made. Forest cutting on a large scale, resumed by Freitag in 1848 and continued since by Yevdokimov, had made the Russian line safe, and at the same time given increased facilities for gaining access to such native strongholds as still remained intact.

He achieved many victories in the years to come. His

---

9. Akti, x, pp. 745-52, where the history of Russo-Persian relations at this time is given in detail.

early education played a vital role in developing his fine qualities and brought forth his hidden potential. His miraculous achievements had much to do with his early education and as such a brief mention of it would not be irrelevant.

Bariantisky stayed at his home till he was five years old. In the next two years, his body was trained for all types of exertion: physical exercises, riding, cold water baths and such other hardships, improved his physical stamina. Later on he was to learn languages. In those days, the aristocracy in Russia did not lay much emphasis on learning Russian. However Bariantinsky was taught Russian apart from French, Greek and Arabic. He knew poetry, eloquence, mathematics, engineering, practical agriculture and woodwork. The latter skills were taught to inculcate practical abilities in him. After learning these various skills, Bariatinsky was sent on a five year tour of Europe. This tour took him to all countries of Europe and was meant to create a broader vision and maturer understanding in him. A group of tutors accompanied him on his tour: a chemist, a doctor, a botanist and mechanic were also attached with the party. It was expected that the tour would help him to possess the practical knowledge and a true appreciation of the varied problems of life.

After his European tour, the party accompanied him on another two year travel through Russia. After he had finished his seven year journeys, he had to supervise agriculture. His father's will explicitly forbade him to accept a job in the army, foreign service or that of a courtier. He may join interior ministry or finance ministry. His father had made his son his heir and all property and wealth were to go to him, after his death. It seems so strange that ignoring his father's will, he decided to join the army. Owing to close associations with the royal family, the queen came to know of it and supporting the views of Bariatinsky commissioned him in his own regiment. Bariatinsky had an adventurous spirit. He wanted to go to the Caucasus and experience its thrilling life. He was appointed in a Cossack regiment under which he displayed his gallantry and was the lone survivor of a campaign and though seriously wounded, kept on fighting till last. The Tsar awarded him a golden sabre as a reward. For the next fifteen years, he continued fighting, many times returning wounded. The Russian novelist Tolstoy writes about him, "Commanders, officers and men all love him immensely. No doubt he is a great commander."

Bariatinsky's education had created in him an understanding of affairs and he was a good judge of circumstances. It was because of his able governorship that he could win the war which had been a mere series of earlier defeats.

The Imam's difficulties
The Chechens inhabiting the contested land now found their position intolerable, for the Russian victories made their lives miserable. The Russians used to harass and persecute these poor people for siding with the Imam. He allowed these people to migrate to inner Chechnya. With the passage of time, the Cossack line had been extended

southwards, as most of the peasants bordering the area where the Russians invaded had migrated towards more secure southern territories. Thus the Russians could tighten their circle around Daghestan. The line of Cossack colonies was strengthened while the felling of the forest trees and the construction of strategic roads had made the Russian line of communication more secure.

Leo Tolstoy

It was at this time that Count Leo Tolstoy, serving as an officer in the 20th Artillery Brigade, gained that knowledge of Cossack life and Caucasian warfare so brilliantly set forth in some of his military stories. "The Cossacks", a tale of 1852, gives a vivid picture of life on the line in those days, facing Chechnya.

Tolstoy was transferred to Sevastopol at the beginning of the Crimean war. He also wrote another novel, "Haji Murad", based on the life of Haji Murad.[10]

On 28 March 1854, France and England declared war on Russia, and peace was not concluded until 30 March 1856. In these days any hostilities on the part of Persia would have changed the situation. At one time the situation had become so precarious that General Road, the civil governor of the Caucasus, had proposed in April 1854 that, in view of Persia's attitude, all the Russian garrisons from Daghestan

---

10. A movie based on this novel has also been produced, under the same title.

should be withdrawn. This would have left the whole of the eastern Caucasus from the Soulak to the Aras to Imam Shamil! At this hour, when Persia would have played a historic role, it betrayed the independence movement in Daghestan and in a secret convention which was concluded at Teheran, on September 29, 1854, Persia agreed to remain absolutely neutral while the war lasted in return for the abandonment by Russia of her claim to the balance of the old war indemnity.

The Shah of Iran's neutrality was bought bribed. This agreement remained secret and went a long way in helping the Russian government.

Russian hostages

Meanwhile Imam Shamil made a skillful use of the war to maintain his influence amongst his compatriots. He invaded Dajarobielokani districts, east of Georgia, in August 1853 with 15,000 of his followers. However the Russian commander proved his mettle by crossing five peaks and defeated the Imam's force in a pitched battle. In another effort against the Russians, 500 of the Imam's men fell martyrs.

Imam Shamil had not forgotten his son Jamaluddin who had been treacherously taken away from him by the Russians. In order to effect the release of his son, he had tried for long but it was all in vain. Now it so happened that a small party under Gazi Muhammad raided the country residence of Princess Orbeliani and carried off the whole family. The princess along with the granddaughter of the last Tsar of Georgia, George XII, were now to be released by exchanging them for the Imam's son. The capture of his distinguished family aroused grave concern and negotiations were begun for their release. The emperor consented to give up Jamaluddin in exchange. Imam Shamil also demanded ransom as he knew that the Russians will have to agree to any proposal. After long negotiations the Russians agreed to pay 40,000; and on 10 March 1865 the exchange was effected with much solemnity on the banks of the little river Mitchik.

Jamaluddin, now a lieutenant in a Russian Lancer regiment, was accompanied by Prince Tchavtchavadze, husband of the princess, and Baron Nicolay, commanding the Russian forces. These three, with an escort of thirty men and a cart carrying the ransom, came forward to the riverside. Gazi Muhammad, with an equal number of Murids, advanced on the opposite bank with the *arbas* (two-wheeled carts) containing the captives. Then, Jamaluddin, accompanied by two Russian officers and the cart with the money, crossed the river to the left bank, the princesses to the right, where they took their places in the carriages that had been brought from Grozny for them.

Jamaluddin was made to change his Russian uniform for the Daghestani dress, and then rode up the hill to where Imam Shamil sat, with Gazi Muhammad and Daniel Sultan on either side, surrounded by his Murids, under a huge blue cotton umbrella. When his son drew near he embraced him, weeping; but the event he had so longed for had in it the seeds of a bitter disappointment.

The fate of Jamaluddin was indeed a sad one. Brought up from the age of twelve in St. Petersburg and recruited in the Russian army, he was now a stranger to his own father, an alien in the land of his birth, and totally unable to resume his place amongst his own people. Furthermore, there was little sympathy between his fellow countrymen and himself, and they soon began to look upon him with suspicion and dislike. Even Imam Shamil was estranged when he found his son imbued with Russian ideas and convinced of Russia's might to an extent that led him to counsel surrender. After a short time Jamaluddin was sent to live in Karata, the chief village of the community of that name, the residence of his younger brother, Gazi Muhammad, and a place of scenic beauty. But neither the charming scenery nor his brother's loving care could reconcile him to the change in his environment. He grew melancholy, fell into a decline, and within three years died.

The Imam's routine
The ruins of Shamil's residence at Veden are still visible on the right bank of the stream.

In those days it was a place of considerable size, Shamil's own quarters consisting of several rooms. The Imam received his visitors in the guest room, built for this purpose.

Of the many guests who were admitted to the Imam's table, the most notable was Daniel, the former sultan of Elisou, whose daughter was married to Shamil's son, Gazi Muhammad. But the only guest who was never failed to be welcomed was a very plain black and white cat, the gift of a Russian deserter. For this animal Shamil had a great affection, and, when at Veden, he never dined without his four-footed friend nor began his own meal until he had prepared hers. The table was small and low. The feline and her master sat on the floor on opposite sides. During the siege, while Shamil was in the neighbouring forest, the cat grew melancholy and, in spite of all Gazi Muhammad could do for her, died. He buried her with much honour, even pronouncing *Al-Fatihah* over her grave; but Imam Shamil, when he heard that his little favourite was dead, took it much to heart, exclaiming, "Now it will go badly with me."

The domestic servants at Veden were prisoners of war, both Muslim and Christian, the former continuing to serve voluntarily though Imam Shamil had given them their liberty. Abdul Rahman, son of Imam Shamil's old friend Jamaluddin, writes of him: "He was very good and kind to common people, to servants, beggars, and even prisoners. He was convinced that the prayers of the poor were acceptable to God, and when setting out on a campaign he would call them together, give them money, cotton cloth, etc., and beg them to pray for the success of his enterprise".

Shamil had six wives in all. Fatimah, daughter of Abdul Aziz who cured him of his wounds of Untsukul, was the mother of his three sons. Another, Dajvgarad of Ghimry, was killed by a Russian bullet at Akhulgo, together with her infant son; Zeidat was the daughter of Jamaluddin of Kazi Kumukh, Shamil's teacher and friend. Aminah was a pretty Kist (mountain Chechen); Shouanet, the beautiful Armenian who had been taken captive during Akhverdi Mohoma's raid on Mozdok in 1840. Of all Shamil's wives she was the one he loved most. For him she abandoned the religion of her fathers and became a sincere and zealous Muslim. When her brother, a rich merchant, offered 10,000 roubles ransom for her, Shamil replied that he would not take a million, and Shouanet would not have abandoned him for as much or more.

When the dreaded day came and Imam Shamil was surrounded on Gunib by the victorious Russian army, the fate of his family was for a short time doubtful. The very worst might happen. But Shouanet trembled only for him; when permission was given to share his captivity she did so without hesitation, though she might have regained her freedom and returned to her own home and people.

9

The Last Encounter

Russia had ample time and resources to launch a fresh offensive in the Caucasus. Once her borders were free from the dangers of foreign invasion, she could attend to the looming danger of the guerrilla forces of Imam Shamil.

Prince Bariatinsky was now appointed as Viceroy and commander-in-chief of Caucasus and Millotine, as his Russian position in Caucasus had improved. The borders were secure after the construction of an elaborate chain of cantonments and forts. The extensive cutting of trees had cleared the roads through jungles and the dangers faced hitherto by various campaigns were over. However the major reason was the declining influence of the Imam amongst the tribesmen.

Difficulties faced by Murid movement

A stagnant period is demoralizing for any movement. As long as the movement is at its peak, the members' morale is high. Every success brings new satisfaction and the zeal to sacrifice increases.

On the other hand if the period of struggle gives way to stagnation, the morale goes down, mutual disensions arise and the standstill gives way to deterioration. This is a period of great turmoil and perhaps the most difficult time for the leader of any movement. He faces the dilemma of maintaining the zeal of the movement at a speed that his comrades neither wear themselves out nor become lethargic. The comrades used to say that they had come all that way to the mountains to fight whereas there were no signs of any fighting. If the irregular warfare had continued, these people would have remained busy and it might have contributed towards the movement as a whole.

The leader of a movement sees things from a different angle. He has a long range programme and as such comrades who lack the farsighted vision do not agree with him. They tend to be impatient. Till such time the leader of a movement keeps the candle of faith burning in the heart of his companions, the movement progresses. No sooner the comrades start losing faith in the leadership, scepticism overwhelms determination and hard work. This situation is far worse than a hundred attacks by the enemy forces. The whole edifice of the movement becomes moth-eaten and it cannot stand stresses and strains.

One may similarly view initial chapters of the history of Islam. Till such time as the companions of our Holy Prophet (peace be upon him) kept on fighting, they were on the rise. But no sooner did the conquests stop, internal dissensions started and the Muslims arrayed themselves against each other. This interpretation of history may appear strange to some people but if one analyses the history of early Islamic period, many mysteries may thus unfold themselves.

The period of peace and prosperity after the campaigns have successfully ended is extremely difficult for any movement. Struggle—and constant struggle alone—can preserve a movement.

The Murid movement prospered as long as there were constant successes in the battlefield. The enemy faced defeats after defeats and now if the tempo slackened, only the Russians could profit. For the guerrilla forces, it could be as well fatal situation.

The Russian designs

Half a century of Russian failure had taught them a lesson. They had deeply analysed the causes of their defeats. The major defeat of Russian war machine was that troops had to depend for various orders and administrative problems, on a chief sitting hundreds of miles away and he too in turn had to obtain orders from the commander-in-chief or viceroy. This situation was obviously precarious for any campaign. The left flank in the north was being commanded by a general sitting away in Stavropol.

The new commander-in-chief Bariatinsky divided the whole of Caucasian army into five commands. Each commander was given full powers and was made answerable to him personally. Three of these commands were situated in Eastern Caucasus. The army at the left flank faced Chechnya. The army facing the Caspian Sea, including the south eastern range, had to reach the heart of Daghestan at the same time. The first two armies had to reach Chechnya in the south east and join hands with the third army in the valley of river Andy. The remaining two armies were kept reserve and were ready to be called in the time of need. The extraordinary successes of Vodeekomov made certain changes in the programme inevitable. The recent victories increased the authority of his command.

In 1857, according to the plan, Vodeekomov's army on the left flank had captured the lower Chechnya. On the other side the Daghestan force had conquered the areas of Slato and Okh under the command of Prince Orbeliani. The commander of Lezginian Line, Baron Worsky, had constructed roads in all these areas. The jugles had also been opened up and tracks made. Burtunai was captured and the staff quarters of the Russian Daghestani foot regiment had been shifted there.

400 Murids and two *naibs* fell martyrs during this Russian campaign. A notable thing in this campaign was the Russian use of rifles. The Murids had rifles on a limited scale even earlier. A road leading to Vileem was constructed by cutting the jungles and a new fort had been constructed at Burtunai in which four battalions were living.

Bariatinsky's measures

In 1858 Bariatinsky had deprived the Imam of an important stronghold, as the upper valley had been captured by the princes. This was a point of strategic importance as the Imam was now cut off from the whole of the Caucasus on the west of Sarawagon. Now only northern Daghestan, Andy and Atkheria were under the direct control of the Imam.

On the other hand there was no way out for the tribes of

Chechnya situated on the west of Argun and Angoushi and between the river Argun and Terek, except to submit to the Russians. With the blockade of the eastern Caucasus, the Imam was facing a precarious situation.

The Imam had been defeated in many pitched battles. His *naibs* had fallen martyrs and many districts had accepted unconditional surrender to Russia. However for a talented leader like Imam Shamil, having a large Murid army, it was not difficult to face the Russian onslaught, in the forest clad mountains, if the local population sided with him and helped their resources. It was only the latter condition which failed the Imam.

The Russian advance

Imam Shamil still maintained his ties with tribes who had submitted to the Russians. He had an effective spying network. However, Vodeekomov played such a trick that the Imam could not determine the direction of his attack till it came. He knew about the advance and preparation of his forces but he reckoned and even the forces were told that Akhtouri, twenty miles east of Argun, was the target. Only the commander and a few staff officers knew about the real distinction. It was such a well guarded secret that the two columns who left Barogal on the night of 15 January did not know their destination. After travelling the whole night crossing the snow clad peaks they reached the left bank of Argun near a tower. Here they were to enter a narrow gorge when they saw a third column on the left bank of the river led by Vodeekemov personally. This last column had to face tough resistance from the brave mujahidin of Chechnya near the narrow gorge. The mujahidin stuck to their position till such time the fact dawned on them that two other columns were also advancing from the other side of the river and if they did not take immediate action, there position would be in imminent danger. In order to save themselves from being encircled, they withdrew.

With the capture of this pass, the local population which had up to this time defied the Russians, now welcomed the arrival of these troops. The pass was considered unsurmountable. Once it passed on the Russians hands, the local population was demoralised. A chronicler writes that the local populace started selling their produce to the Russians and in a short while, the whole pass turned itself into a bazaar.

It is said that when the Imam was informed about the Russian capture of the pass, his eyes filled with tears. He had anticipated that the end was not far off. Even at that time a large group of mujahidin were with him. Why did he not try to launch a counter offensive? Many thousand Daghestanis were still with him, and before the Russians could capture the whole territory, the Imam could have defeated the Russians. At this hour of crisis the Imam took no action.

On the other side, the Russians had started cutting the trees on a large scale and hundreds of trees were cut down every day. The noise of the Russian exes was far more demoralising than the thunder of Russian artillery.

1,400 yards of space had been cleared upto the right of Dargun Rokh. This peak was 6,000 feet high and at a distance of ten miles, the Russians could see the house of the Imam in the plains of Veden. Forest were being cleared in other parts as well, bridges were being constructed and even a fort had been constructed at Argunski. The feeble artillery of the Imam could not breach the fort up to April. The Russian commander left a substantial number of forces in this fort and withdrew towards Vodeshinko and Grozny. The winter campaign had been successful and now the forces were going back for rest.

By 1858, all preparation were completed, and once again the Russian forces entered Argun pass, but now much had changed. Conditions were dramatically different. The giant beech trees had been cleared, the fords and rivers had bridges, roads were everywhere and there were no mujahidin to hinder the forces. Six months earlier the Russians had faced immense difficulties in going over this route. This had raised the morale of the Russian commander.

The route ahead of this was quite difficult. The river passed through thousands feet of deep gorges and at many places could not be crossed. This path was so difficult that if the mujahidin had faced the Russian at any point, the Russian advance could have been halted. In the meanwhile the spies informed Vodeekemov that the mujahidin were busy constructing blockades and trenches in order to halt the Russian advance. The Russian general was however not one of those who had believed in frontal attack alone. He let his armies pass on the right side of the river and then all of a sudden made his left flank go over to the left bank of the river and conquered the height of Miskindagh with little resistence. He descended from this place, reached the village of Varanda, where the villagers submitted to him. He now again crossed the river and constructed a temporary fort at Danakh village and joined it with the fort of Argunsko with the help of a new road. Half of the road leading to Shaton was already in the hands of the Russians. With a little more effort they were successful in capturing the rest of the route. By the end of July the Russian crossed this part also, ousted the defenders of Varanda and stormed the heights which had cut off Shaton with other places in the valley. There was no further resistance in this area.

The Russian advance column crossed Khanti river and entered Shaton. The Russians now attended to the establishment of communications between Zonakh and Argunsko. The local village folk had already been impressed by the Russian victory. Now they lost all hope. They had realised that the Russians are going to win and had already transferred their loyalties.

The disloyalty of local population

Nothing succeeds like success. The Russian victories at one place led to similar victories at others. Like the Kufic people, the local villagers joined their swords with the Russians. At many a place they openly betrayed the Imam, and being more loyal than the king himself, killed the compatriots of the Imam. The *naib* of the Imam was imprisoned by those at Etom fort and his brother and other Murids were killed. The Russians were sent a message to occupy the fort and its weapons. Argun's upper reaches were still with the Imam and a new route of reaching Daghestan had opened up.

Orbeliani had been replaced by Wrangel and in the

meanwhile he had captured the rest of Gambeet and Okh and advanced through Daghestan. On the other side, Riveesky had advanced towards Deevoz like last year and once again put the whole area to sword and fire in the "best Russian traditions". He was himself killed while attacking the village of Keetori, but he had finished his task. When Prince Melehof advanced, he did not find any obstacle except the mountainous paths and the jungle.

The siege of Nazran

Imam Shamil launched a great offensive during the second campaign of Argun. The people of Nazran, who were previously the allies of the Russians, sought help from the Imam and raised the banner of freedom. The Imam crossed Khanti and despite the volleys of Russian artillery, reached the plains. At Akhoki, however, he had to suffer great losses and withdraw. As Nazran could only be reached through a long and torturous route, he now retreated.

In the meanwhile the Russian troops had reached Nazran to suppress rebellion against them. Nazran was besieged, six guns of Russian cavalry razed the village. Four leaders were hanged and forty children were taken to Caucasus as hostages, where they were beaten mercilessly. When these children returned, they had grown up and their hearts were full of enmity against the Russians. They were once again ready to revolt.

The Imam tried to distract the Russian attention, so that they could withdraw and now he attacked Nazran at the head of 4,000 mounted Murids. Here too he had to retreat with many losses. 370 Murids fell martyrs, whereas on the other hand only 16 Russians were killed and 26 soldiers wounded.

The causes of Russian victory

At the end of the war Prince Bariatinsky wrote the following about Vodeekemov which explains the new scheme of Russian warfare. He says:

Vodeekemov never allowed the enemy to fight at a place where it enjoyed an advantageous position. The Imam's most important positions fell merely because of well planned manouevre. Akhulgo Saltees, Ghergheeble and Tokh had cost thousands of Russian life whereas, in Veden where Shamil had concentrated all his might, only 26 of our men were killed or wounded. Three things helped us win the war. Firstly we fought a systematic warfare, secondly our generals committed no tactical mistake, and thirdly, the arming of Caucasian army with the latest weapons. These three things paved the way for our victory. The mountain dwellers could not be conquered by battles. Constant warfare had raised their morals to an extent that a few dozen of their men were able to check the advance of our big columns, and few bullets fired by them caused more damage than hundreds of bullets fired by us. The battle means a sense of equal power. However once they did not get a chance to fight, their morale fell, so long as there was a chance for a war they would have prepared again despite defeat but once they had to disperse without fighting, their morale lowered and they surrendered. One of the main reasons of Shamil's dwindling power was that his forces gathered at one place and they had to disperse without fighting. Nowhere was there a regular battle. In the last ten years of regular campaigns, nowhere did the Tsarist soldiers suffer great losses. During the Caucasian campaigns, these years were the least bloody.

Desertion of Imam's companions

The Russian victories on all fronts had demoralised the masses and they did not have the courage and determination to fight. The same people who had fought till their last against the Russians and had not accepted defeat at any cost were now submitting without any battle waged against them. It all seemed very strange but this is the psychology of defeat.

The constant victories of Russians had shaken the morale fibre of these tribes and they were no longer dauntless brave and heroic warriors. Even prior to this, they had submitted to the Russians but then it was in the desperate conditions when a large number of them had already been killed. Never had they submitted without resistance on a large scale.

Techeria, Taborloi and Ukhis upper reaches had severed their loyalties with the Imam and had accepted the suzerainty of Russia. The inhabitants of Untsakh in the south and other districts situated on the northern slopes had also surrendered. Even the closest comrades of the Imam had forsaken him—Daniel Sultan once again joined hands with the Russians. Even Gazi Sultan Keebat Mohoma of Tiliti considered further resistance futile and not only accepted the Russian hegemony himself but also arrested the Gazi Aslan of Sodekhar, one of the most fiery workers of the Murid movement, and handed him over to the Russians.

On 14 July Bariatinsky met Vodeekemov in his camp across Vedan and now the final onslaught started. Forty thousand troops and forty eight guns accompanied this advancing column. The Imam did not sit idle in this hour of great trial. He kept his composure and his morale remained high. He never despaired. The constant success of the Russians, the desertion of his closest comrades, the surrender of whole provinces, the superior number of the Russian forces and the realization that they are being led by a general of extraordinary calibre—nothing depressed him. He did all he could in those adverse circumstances with every bit of the indefatigable energy he had always possessed.

The Imam once left the mountains of Chechnya and entered Daghestan. He did not rest for a moment and spent entire days and nights to strengthen the defensive positions. During his stay at Etkali, he fortified the place and after strengthening the defences of other areas north of Andy made the river route for the columns of Wrangel and Vodeekemov unpassable. He asked for reinforcements from the surrounding areas. However, all these preparations were in vain, as Vodeekemov, on knowing these preparations, scaled the mountain at Andy and arrived at the mountain opposite Bultakh. When people of the village Andy saw the Russian bayonets flashing on the mountain top, they were disheartened. The people of Tabarlof sent a delegation to Bariatinsky to allow them to return to their village under Russian escort. Despite the exhortations of Imam Shamil's *naib* Dabir, they all surrendered. The next day the people of Andy also deserted the Imam. Gazi Muhammad, the Imam's son, seeing that he was being encircled, left the fort of Atkali along with eleven guns. The troops under the command of Wrangel soon took over the areas of Kosubo and Avaria and the whole of the district accepted Russian rule.

The Russians now did not face any resistance in the

whole area. The fort of Olu surrendered on its own. This fort, situated near Gherghebil as it was, had defied the might of Russians for a very long time. Even the unsurmoutable Ukh fell into the Russian hands.

On 28 July, Keebat Mohoma reached Gloti and taking the Russian vanguard, led by General Racos, reached his native village Tiliti. On seeing this situation, the upper Avar areas also surrendered. On 7 August, Daniel Sultan who had handed over Arib and other forts to the Russians, arrived at the camp of Bariatinsky to seek forgiveness.

The Imam observed all this. Even his closest comrades had joined the Russians. His movement had withered like the frost beaten leaves in autumn and his brave soldiers had disappeared like the snow on the summits in spring. He reached Gunib along with his family. On the route the women of a village were known to be of bad repute. Akwakh (this aoul was ill reputed because of not being hospitable throughout the area) stole away some luggage from the Imam's train and Keebat Mohoma's companion looted the rest of it near Ronga. The person who was nearest and dearest to the Imam did not spare his honour today.

Even in these tragic circumstances when the whole of the country was hostile to the Imam, and when even his dearest friends had turned out to be his bitterest foes, the people of Gunib remained faithful to the Imam. The poor peasants welcomed the Imam. They knew fully well that to protect the Imam would mean disaster for them. They knew that the Russians would trample their village and yet they decided to side with the Imam till their last breath.

There were only 400 comrades with the Imam. In this

hopeless situation, the Imam decided to strengthen his defences in the village. These people dug trenches, built strongholds and worked day and night to strengthen their last defence. The Imam used to recite these verses of an Arab poet, which befitted his present conditions.

> I considered myself attached to my brothers like the joints of chains, even they have turned into my enemies. I considered them sharp like arrows. They were sharp arrows but have stung my heart.

On 9 August, Wrangel arrived, and the siege started. The next day, Prince Bariatinsky, Vodeekemov, his staff officers, the Russian bodyguards and the native militia went out to inspect the area which had surrendered. Agalee, Sgreetal, Tinkat and Kheetta were the various places through which this train passed and now they reached Unstukul and Ghimry. Here Bariatinsky left the Russian guards and took his staff officers and the inhabitants of Kosubo and Avaria along with him. Two days afterwards, he met Keebat Mohoma at Tiliti and dined with him. The same night he encamped at the base of Temovan mountain. On 18 August he rejoined Wrangel on the summit of Gunib after inspecting Raja and Takh. During the whole journey, he was welcomed everywhere.

Last refuge
Imam Shamil's last refuge can be located with the aid of a map. On all sides the rocks are raised to the height of 3,000 to 5,000 feet, whereas on the west, the wall-like rocks reach a height of 7,718 feet. Amongst these walls, the ground is flat like the lower base of a cup. There are bastion-like

mountains on all sides and there is an abundance of water. Maize, barley and all kinds of fruit are grown here. During the days when there was no long range artillery, the place was as secure as a fort. If there were sufficient number of defenders it was not difficult to make the place impregnable. But the Imam had only 400 comrades. The place was stormed from ten different positions by companies and at many places by battalion strength. It would not be difficult to imagine the situation in which 400 persons had to defend an area of 11 miles circumference. If there were four thousand troops, it would have been difficult for the Russians to conquer it, but there was no question of its defence with 400 men alone. At least one column out of ten would have stormed and once it had to be checked, other positions would have remained undefended.

Imam Shamil had taken position on the mountain opposite Kara river, in his tent, and was inspecting the defence preparations. He must have heard the shoutings of joy in Bariatinsky's camp. Thirty years before, he had started working for the glory of Islam in this very area. He had been trying to crush the Russian might and he had been successful in achieving his cherished goal. However, now the tables were turned against him. He now clearly saw that the hour of martyrdom was approaching fast. He was determined to fight till the end. He had dedicated his life to the sacred task of fighting the *giaour*. He had faced both disasters, and triumphs in his life. He had defeated the Russians and had been defeated by them as well. He had worked with all his heart and soul in the life of the first Imam and it was only a miracle which saved him when the first Imam had fallen martyr in the battlefield. He remained loyal to Hamzad as well. He could have been installed as the Imam but did not do so. He had led the Murid forces since 1834, and had ruled over the whole of Daghestan.

Now once after a lifetime of struggle and years of unfailing endeavours he was facing tremendous odds; the defeat seemed certain. His conscience was satisfied that he did not fail his cause. Every impartial historian would agree on this. In fact the failure of his movement was not the result of any of misdeeds on his part. Circumstances had taken such a turn that were beyond his control.

The Imam had failed but a thousand successes can be sacrificed for it. If one estimates the heavy odds against which he led his movement, it seems miraculous that he survived for so long. There were not only external factors hindering him, but the internal situation also did not favour him.

He had not only to fight the overwhelming numbers of the Tsar's armies and the vast resources which the empire had; he had also to deal with the internal dissensions and tribal rivalries. The circumstances were so adverse that he could not fully encounter once nor crush another. If the Caucasus had been inhabited by the people of the same tribe, race or who speak the same language, his task could have been much easier. These people—all Muslims—were still ready to shed each other's blood.

It was not easy to bring peace to a land which had not seen anything except blood feuds for many centuries. If the tribes were united, the Imam might have been able to defeat even a greater imperialist power than Russia. The tribes remained united only temporarily till such time that the war with Russia was at its peak. No sooner there was lull, disintegration set in. The Imam had imposed law and order amongst the tribes. Now it seems an irony of fate that the discipline which he had enforced amongst the tribes through the Murid movement was utilised by the Russians. The Imam once said at a later moment that what took him so many years to achieve, the Russians gained in no time.

He knew that the tribes can never be united unless the *Shari'ah* are enforced. He had to be firm in order to achieve this. He preached and persuaded the people, many a time he had to use force. He achieved many victories and yet the forces of disintegration were at work even in the period of greatest discipline and peace. The people who had adhered to *adat* for a long period, considered it burdensome to adhere to the laws of the *Shari'ah*. The laws enforced by the *naibs* were not welcomed by them.

Another factor of great importance was the fact that the war had been prolonged to an extent where it told upon the perseverance of the local population. There was hardly any family where a husband, a father or a brother had not fallen martyr. Even whole families had perished and entire villages razed to the ground. For years there had been no cultivation of the soil and nobody had looked after the orchards.

All this happened in Daghestan where the Imam lived and where his word was law. Chechnya suffered even more. These people had to migrate at the hands of their own friends and relations. On the other hand, Russia was spending large sums of money on these people. She required an army of guides, scouts, militia, cavalrymen, spies and traitors. In order to achieve her domination she was spending huge sums of money on the poor people, who had known nothing else except destitution, poverty and hunger. If one takes all this into account, one is not astonished at the Imam's failure. Rather, one is amazed at the fact that the Murid movement could be sustained for such a long period. Thirty years of constant warfare had demoralised the people. This was a burden beyond their capacity, The attitude of the people does not seem so strange if one keeps this situation in view.

The Russian attack

It was a frosty morning of 25 August 1859, when there was fog all around. The Russians launched their attack. The local guides were directing the attack and the battalions had launched an all-out attack. The Imam retreated towards the villages. The Murids put up a heroic defence. At one position 100 Murids fell fighting till the end. At another stronghold a few Murids tried to halt an attack of battalion strength—they also fell. Brave women also fought desperately and embraced martyrdom.

Bariatinsky waited to take the Imam alive. Before attacking the village he tried to negotiate for peace. If the Imam had been alone, he would have chosen to die but here were his children and wives and apart from them were those faithful village folk who had given protection to him when the whole of Daghestan and Chechnya had turned into his enemy and people who were thirsty for his blood. These were the people who had worked day and night to construct the defences of the village. They were determined to fight till last and save the Imam. If there was a general attack not a single soul in the village would have been saved.

The Imam had much consideration for the old men, women, children and his loyal comrades. He sent two of his comrades to negotiate peace.

The Russians demanded unconditional surrender on which Imam Shamil could not agree. Finally, Colonel Lazarov, who knew the Imam personally, arrived in the village and promised to save the life of every peasant in the village. Now, Shamil rode on the horse, but hardly had he gone a few paces ahead when the Russian soldiers, seeing their time old adversary amongst them, started clapping. He stopped, pulled his reigns and was about to return back to the village, when Lazarov acted on the spur of the moment. Considering the situation, he rushed towards the Imam and explained that the soldiers clapped to welcome him. The colonel brought him along. He had fifty Murids along with him, the remnants of the thousands of mujahidin.

When Imam Shamil drew closer to Bariatinsky, his face was still stiff and he had the stare of an eagle. Bariatinsky assured him of the safety of his compatriots and his family. The next day he was sent to Temir-Khan-Shura, from where he proceeded to Moscow followed by his family.

In this last battle, 180 Russians were killed and wounded. On the other side only 50 Murids out of 400 had survived the attack.

Imam Shamil remained at Kluge till 1869. Later on, he was shifted to Khiva on his own request. From here he was allowed to proceed on the Hajj pilgrimage, where he breathed his last on 4 February 1871 in Madinah, the city of the Holy Prophet. Thus ended the brilliant and dramatic career of a life which had been dedicated to the battlefield and the stories of whose valour are still sung in the aouls of Daghestan.

Appendix

The Song of the Death of Khochbar

A messenger came from the Avar Khan to summon Khochbar of Ghedatl.[1]

"Shall I go to Khounzakh, O my mother?"

"Go not, my darling, go not! The grief for blood that is spilt lasts long; the Khans—may they perish—set traps for men."

"Not so, I will go; or the vermin of Khounzakh will think that I fear them; the despised Noutsal will call me a coward."

So Khochbar rode to Khounzakh, driving before him an

---

1. Ghedatl, or Gheed, was an Avar community to the south of the khanate and, owing to its favourable situation in a wide basin surrounded on all sides by mountains, with a comparatively good climate and fertile soil, one of the strongest and most flourishing villages. The inhabitants were frequently at war with their cousins of Akhwakh and of the khanate, and extended their frontier at the former's expense. They were noted for their horned cattle and farm produce, which they sold to their neighbours and to the Russian garrisons. The name is now only given to a small aoul above the aoul near the left bank of the Avar Koisu, at the foot of the Bogos range, having three peaks of over 13,000 feet.

ox, a gift for the Khan; a ring he took with him to give the Khan's wife.

"Hail! Noutsal of Avaria!"

"Khochbar of Ghedatl, hail! Thou art come at last, O wolf that rendest the sheep! Thou art here, O enemy of the Avars."

While the Noutsal and Khochbar were talking, the crier cried aloud:

"Let him who has a cart bring pine-wood from the forest; let him who has none load his ass with it; let him who has neither arba nor donkey carry it on his own back; our enemy Khochbar has fallen into our hands; let us build a pyre and burn him!"

The crier ceased, and six men sprang upon Khochbar, and bound, him. On the long hill-side of Khounzakh they made such a blaze that the very rock grew red-hot beneath it. They brought Khochbar to the fire; they brought to it his gallant bay steed; they slaughtered it with their swords; they broke in twain his sharp-pointed spear, and threw the pieces into the flames—the hero winked never an eye!

"Come now, Khochbar, sing us something; it is said thou art a a master of song. Play us somewhat on the lime-wood cithern; it is said thou playest well!"

"Well indeed can I sing; but my mouth is gagged. Well indeed can I play; but my hands are bound!"

The young men cried that Khochbar should be freed; but the old men said, "Wolf-deeds we fear from a wolf!"

The young men had their way; the hero was unbound.

"Listen now, men of Khounzakh; I will sing you a song; and thou, O Khan, interrupt me not!" He sings to the cithern:

> Who but I clambered in through your window, and carried off the silk trousers of your favourite wife? Who but I took the silver bracelets from the white arms of your complacent sisters! Who but I cut the throat of your tame Tour.[2] There, above, are the sheepfolks; who drove the sheep away? Why are they empty? There, below, is the stable; who drove the horses off? Where are they now? Lo! on the house tops, the widows! Who killed their husbands and made them such? Orphans I see around me! Who slew their sires and orphaned them? None can count the number of those who have died by my hand, in the fields! In the forest! I have slaughtered no less than three-score men of your tribe! These are deeds, O Noutsal, worthy of Fame; but to take a man by fraud and kill him—what shall we say of that?

While Khochbar sang and played, the two little sons of the Khan came round and sat at his feet. Snatching them up suddenly, one in each hand, the hero leapt into the flames.

> Why shriek, ye Noutsal cubs. Do not I burn with you?
> Why squeal, ye piglings. Did not I too love the Light?
> Alas! for my gallant bay, that trampled so oft the heels of the flying Avars! Alas! for my pointed lance, that pierced full oft the breasts of the Noutsal's henchmen!
> Weep not, mother mine—not vainly your darling dies!
> Let not my sisters greet—I perish gloriously!
> There was scraping of viols and beating of drums. from morn till noon; Khochar of Ghedatl was taken!
> There was weeping and wailing when noon was past; the Avar princes had perished in the flames!

---

2. Mountain goat.

The date of this occurrence—historical no doubt—as to the main facts, is unknown. The reference to a pinewood near Khounzakh is a proof of its antiquity; for not a tree of any sort grows near, nor has it done so in human memory. The barrenness, indeed, of the neighbourhood, is after the chasm into which the Tobot plunges just below the soul, its most striking feature.

The whole song is highly characteristic— Khochbar's pride and courage; his stoical firmness when his favourite horse is killed, his trusty spear broken; the vaunting strain of his death-song, with its string of insults, based on truth, but purposely exaggerated—are all of nature to excite to the utmost the admiration of the mountaineers: and at the final catastrophe their enthusiasm knows no bounds. It is not difficult to imagine Haji Murad in similar circumstances behaving exactly as Knochbar is said to have done.

What Haji Murad and his companions sang on this occasion is unknown, but the following "Song of the Death of Hamzad" gives a vivid picture of a similar scene, and is interesting as a specimen of Chechen poetry.

The white hawk, flying, overtakes pray and seizes it with her talons. She seizes it—and straightway bathes her beak in blood.

The spotted panther, swift of foot, overtakes his quarry and pounces on it with his mighty claws.

The bold Hamzad, with the gallant horsemen of Ghikh,

crosses to the left bank of the Terek and leaves the river behind him.

The brave Hamzad, has crossed the Terek and entered the Nogai Steppes. He has captured a herd of white horses and again crossed the Terek, driving it before him.

At the dawn of day he crossed it and drove the herd into the brushwood of Shirvan, on the Hill of the Cherkess.

There was danger by day, and the riders were tired. They halted at Shirvan—Koulee and hid their spoil in the thicket.

When he had hidden his booty and his companions in the wood, Hamzad ascended a high Kourgan, and looked through his glass to see if the Russians were coming.

Hamzad looked and sees a numerous band darkening the place where he had forded the Terek. As fast as black clouds driven by the wind that band comes galloping on his traces.

Seeing the multitude he went down from the Kourgan and said to his companions, "They follow as fast as the wind follows the clouds. Be not afraid, we will fight like famished leopards!"

And again he said unto them, "We will slaughter the horses and the cattle, and surround ourselves with them as with a rampart. Then we shall be able to defend ourselves!"

His companions joyfully gave their consent. They cut the throats of the horses and stabled the horned cattle and made a strong fence round about them.

And again Hamzad spoke to his companions and said, "The Naib of Ghikh, Akhverdi Mohoma, stands likewise no doubt with his men on the hill-top.

"When he hears the noise of fighting with the Russians he will fly to our aid like a bird of the air."

But this he said but to hearten his companions.

Hamzad sat down with his riders behind the bloody breakwork and ordered one to keep watch on the enemy. The sentinel stands gazing earnestly.

And lo! A horseman gallops out in front of the crowd—Prince Kagherman—and coming within hail cries out, "What Prince's people are you?"

The warder never utters a word, but repeats the question to Hamzad: "Prince Kagherman wishes to know what prince's people we are!"

Brave Hamzad went out from behind the breakwork and drew near to the horseman.

"What do you want of us!—To know what prince's people you are!"

Hamzad laughed, "We know no princes nor want to; we are riders from Ghikh and came for spoil!"

"Art thou not Hamzad?" asked Kagherman.

"I am Hamzad!"

"It's a pity, Hamzad, that you came here. A Russian band has overtaken you—overtaken and surrounded you. Unless you can grow as of migrant birds and fly up in the air, you cannot escape. The Russian commander has sent me: he will spare you, if you surrender without fighting!"

To this Hamzad answered, "I came not here, O Kagherman, for lack of wealth: I came to witness the death of the *ghazavat*. And were I to surrender to thee, all the people of Ghikh would laugh me to scorn.

"As a wolf tired and hungry longs to reach the forest, as a starving horse and mettlesome the fresh clean meadow—so do my companions thirst for the fight unto death. Not do I fear thee, Kagherman. I laugh at all thy force: for our hope is in God, the all-powerful!"

And again Hamzad said to Kagherman, "Ever we sought booty and gold, but for such a day as this there is nothing so precious as the beautiful black powder!"

And again he said, "Gold is not my wealth today; today the trusty Crimean flint is pure gold!"

Kagherman went back to the Russian commander and told him that Hamzad refused to surrender. And Hamzad returned to his rampart and sat down with his companions.

Then the troops came up and began firing; and Hamzad and his riders fired back.

Thick was the smoke of their firing, and Hamzad said, "May this day be accursed! So hot it is, that we have no shade but that of our swords!"

And again he said, "How thick is the smoke, how dark the day! Our only light is the flash of our guns!"

And again Hamzad said to his companions, "The Houris of Paradise look down on us from their windows in heaven and wonder; they dispute together whose they shall be; and she who falls to the braver of us will vaunt it before her friend—and she who falls to the less brave will blush for shame; she will close the lattice on him and turn away; and if any of you plays the coward this day may his face be black when he stands before God!"

But Hamzad thought in his heart the while that death was upon him; he could hope no more.

High in the heavens he saw the birds flying and called to them, "O birds of the air! Give our last greeting, our ultimate salutation, to the Naib of Ghikh, Akhverdi

Mohoma. Greet also from us the beautiful ones, the damsels fair, and tell them that our proud breasts serve to stop Russian bullets—tell them that our wish was to rest after death in the graveyard at Ghikh, where our sisters would have wept on our tombs, and all the people would have sorrowed—but God grants no such grace. Not the sobbing of our sisters will be heard above us but the howling of famished wolves. No troops will gather round about but a flock of ravens swart.

"And tell them too, on the Cherkess hill, in the land of the Ghaur, bare blades in hand, we lie dead. The ravens pick out our eyes, the wolves tear our flesh!"

The Russian translator tells us that he has more than once seen tears in the eyes of even the most staid amongst the Chechens when listening to the song of Hamzad, who was Abrek (outlaw) from one of the aouls on the Terek. He fled to the mountains in the early years of Muridism, and as leader of small raiding parties continually troubled the Cossack Line, where, thanks to his dauntless courage and thorough knowledge of the locality, his raids were nearly always successful.

Another Chechen death-song may be rendered as follows:

The earth will dry on my grave.
Mother, my Mother!
And thou wilt forget me!
And over me rank grasses wave,
Father, my Father!

Nor wilt thou feel pity for me
When tears cease thy dark eyes to lave,
    Sister, dear Sister!
No more will grief fret thee!
But thou, my Brother the Elder, wilt never forget,
With vengeance denied me!
And thou, my Brother the Younger, wilt ever forget.
Till thou liest beside me!
Hotly thou comest, oh death-bearing ball that I
    spurned,
      For thou wast my Solace!
And thou, black earth, that my battle-steed trampled
    and churned,
Wilt cover my grave!
Cold art Thou, O Death, yet I was thy Lord and
    Master!
My body sinks fast to earth; my Soul to Heaven flies
    faster.

The supreme confidence in the brother as the avenger of blood is worthy of note.

Index

Made in the USA
Monee, IL
08 March 2023

29467041R00122